**Required Reading Range
Course Reader**

Fairchild Books
An imprint of Bloomsbury Publishing Plc

50 Bedford Square
London
WC1B 3DP
UK

1385 Broadway
New York
NY 10018
USA

www.bloomsbury.com

Bloomsbury is a registered trade mark of Bloomsbury Publishing Plc

First edition published in 2005 by AVA Publishing
Second edition published by AVA Publishing 2011
Reprinted by Fairchild Books 2014

British Library Cataloguing-in-Publication Data
A catalogue record for this book is available from the British Library.

ISBN: PB: 978-2-9404-1160-3
ePDF: 978-2-9404-4726-8

Library of Congress Cataloging-in-Publication Data

Noble, Ian; Bestley, Russell.
Visual Research: An Introduction to Research
Methodologies in Graphic Design/Ian Noble, Russell Bestley p. cm.
Includes bibliographical references and index.
ISBN: 9782940411603 (pbk.: alk.paper)
eISBN: 9782940447268
1. Graphic arts–Study and teaching.
2. Graphic arts–Research.
NC997 .N63 2011

Design and text by Russell Bestley and Ian Noble.

Printed and bound in China

Visual Research

2nd edition

Required Reading Range
Course Reader

An Introduction to
Research Methodologies
in Graphic Design

Ian Noble
Russell Bestley

Foreword by Ellen Lupton

Fairchild Books
An Imprint of Bloomsbury Publishing Plc

Contents

Foreword

We tend to think of graphic design in terms of finished goods: a neatly polished poster, logo, layout, or website. Yet graphic design is also a process. A designed artefact emerges from a set of questions whose answers often bump around in the dark before a solution bubbles up to the surface.

Think of this book as a series of answers to questions you may have about graphic design. The questions are posed through concrete examples of work, reproduced with enough depth and scale to let you come safely inside. This is a big book, not because it has to look good on your coffee table but because the ideas are big. The pages have opened their arms wide to make a comfortable place for reading and thinking.

What is research? Research is about looking for something in a focused and systematic way. Scientists and scholars study the published literature and proven results on a topic that they seek to explore; they also set out to create new knowledge through active experiment. The subject of this book is visual research: the emphasis is on making and doing, not reading and writing. Design itself is a form of research, following both measured and intuitive sequences of investigation in order to arrive at new forms and insights.

Does methodology matter? Graphic design is a creative field, not a science. A designer's process tends to be more loopy than linear, tracking back and forth rather than pushing stalwartly forward. Embracing a method, trying it on for size, can help designers shake up their personal habits and dig up fresh results. Pursuing a more structured path can take you to unexpected places. You will find in this book new vocabularies for asking what signs, materials, and images can mean. Rhetoric and semiotics offer ways to consider design's linguistic and social contexts. Mapping and data visualization provide logical means for organizing information and displaying it in illuminating ways. The systematic analysis of a written text can generate richly grained typographies.

This book presents theory as a tool for both synthesis and analysis. The ultimate goal of visual research is to inform form, to infuse signs and surfaces with meaning. A designer is an intellectual who makes things, studying the world of objects, users, and information in order to create living acts of communication. The tools and methods laid out in this book provide a helpful introduction to the methodologies of creative thinking.

Ellen Lupton
Graphic designer, writer, curator and educator

Navigational Aids

There are a number of graphic devices within *Visual Research* to aid reader navigation. The small grid of squares on each verso page (see above left) indicates different sections of the book: chapters, case studies, key concepts and exercises.

Running headlines also give a clear indication of each section, and further colour coding of pages for key concepts and exercises helps to delineate differences. Running glossaries and image captions are also differentiated typographically. Colour bars for chapter opening spreads and the book cover are taken directly through sampling from case study material in each chapter.

Introduction

The title of this book – *Visual Research* – is a term utilized to describe an approach to systematic enquiry and investigation within graphic design. Research in the context of the practice of graphic design can be seen as an underpinning and defining activity, based in large part on the notion of *problem solving* using visual tools and methods.

For many designers, research is a necessary process in exploring how best to arrive at a meaningful and effective solution to the needs of a client or user and the demands of a brief. The understanding of the many factors at work that may influence an individual approach to design problem solving can range from the prosaic and pragmatic to the sophisticated and poetic. This comprehension, born of training, experience, practical skill and personal philosophy, defines the designer and their own personal and idiosyncratic methods of working.

For others, visual research is more related to design as a *problem finding* activity: a practice based not on the search for answers but on the quality and manner of how the questions are asked. In this context, research is not only a working process – it can also be considered an outcome in its own right. This should not be seen as a distinction between pure and applied research, or to suggest that a hierarchy of significance or importance can be placed on either way of working – they are both a significant part of what we might consider contemporary visual communication design and the wide-ranging approaches to the discipline that currently exist.

This book is an attempt to map the field of visual research within the practice of graphic design and to offer an introduction to the research methods and models that have formed the basis of our teaching over the last decade.

Design

The verb *to design* literally means to plan something for a specific role, purpose or effect. The act of *designing*, in terms of visual communication and graphic design, centres on the ways in which a designer addresses practical and theoretical problems through a broad range of often two-dimensional (print-based), but increasingly also three-dimensional or time-based, media, materials and processes.

'Design is an activity of creative reasoning which is dependent upon flexibility of ideas and methodologies informed by an awareness of current critical debates. It ranges between the expressive and functional and can be, for example, stylistically driven or socially motivated.

'Design is an iterative process based upon evaluation and modification… At its core, design involves both analysis and synthesis, and is frequently solution-focused, culminating in the creation of design outcomes as prototypes, models or proposals.'
Subject Benchmark Statements: Art and Design, The Quality Assurance Agency for Higher Education, 2002

Creativity

Creativity is a mental process involving the discovery of new ideas or concepts, or new associations between existing ideas or concepts.

It may also lead to extensions and adaptations of those existing concepts in an original and previously unexplored manner.

Logic

An iterative and reasoned method of human thought that involves the interrogation of a problem, or the creation of a solution to a problem, in a linear, step-by-step manner.

Introduction

The various chapters explore the many aspects of visual research, and are supported throughout with practical examples of projects that illustrate the ideas and processes discussed.

      The work featured in the case studies throughout this new edition was created by some of the students we have taught over recent years. This book and the programme of study that these students undertook are a product of each other. Each designer was encouraged to explore their individual understanding of the role of research within their working methods and the work that they produced. In turn, their work and ideas fed our own understanding of how to develop a meaningful approach to the teaching of graphic design as a research-based activity.

      This new and revised edition of *Visual Research* features a new chapter on Design Literacy, eleven new case studies and additional writing in many of the chapters. This has been supplemented with additional key concepts and a new section accompanying each chapter providing practical exercises based on the ideas discussed. Our approach to the subject of visual research has grown and developed since the first edition, and this updated version of the book represents the further refinement of a key set of methodologies that can be used by graphic designers and visual communicators in the development of clear, purposeful and strategic design solutions.

      What has become clear over recent years is that whilst the environment or context that graphic design exists within is subject to an ever-accelerating rate of change and flux, the key attributes needed in order to function as a designer have remained consistent. These skills are directly related to visual research: methods of working and patterns of enquiry

---

Three useful models of graphic design research are adapted in this book from Christopher Frayling's research approaches and definitions, based on the methodologies, processes, initial aims and final objectives of a design investigation, published in his work 'Research in Art and Design' (1994). Frayling's model is adapted somewhat here, in order to present a clear distinction between different areas of graphic design research and practice.

Models of design research are based on the following themes:

Research about Design
The study of design histories, styles, influences, models and approaches. The main objective is to understand a context or history from different perspectives, such as design criticism and historical research. The goal is related to the deduction of new knowledge and understanding of design as a subject.

Research into Design
The exploration of design methods and practices, including visual testing and experimentation. This research is centred on both understanding the process of design itself and developing new design actions, artefacts or methods.

Research through Design
Research through design involves the development of new artefacts of which the goal is to visually communicate new knowledge, but the practice is not at the centre of the whole research process. The use of graphic design as an instrument for investigating and articulating a particular subject area, which may lie outside of the field of design – as such, this model of design research would include mapping, information design, and editorial approaches to visualizing and categorizing data.

based on what could be called sustainable thinking. This mode of engagement provides a significant focus on what the designer and educator Jan van Toorn has described as *'the designer's field of operation'*. In practice, this is an informed and critical approach to design practice based on rigorous models of exploration and testing that inform both the formal and cultural aspects of the designer's role.

The Structure of the Book

Visual Research is divided into thematic chapters exploring a number of different emphases in relation to research-based graphic design. The case studies reflect a range of practical responses to the themes explored, from visual grammar and design literacy to the relationship between audience and message and the investigation of materials and processes. Key concepts outline ideas and theories that can inform the design process, together with examples of the application of those theories from the perspective of the design practitioner: it is important to reflect on how ideas might be applied and may be of use to the designer in their practice – in the actual *making* of graphic design. Each chapter also includes a series of design exercises, enabling the reader to reflect on the content explored and to further their own understanding of the discipline.

There is not sufficient space available to give credit to the many people who have contributed to our understanding of the subject of this book, but it is important to thank the designers who have given their time and energy in providing the work featured here. This book is the product of many years of collaboration, reflection and debate among graphic design educators, students and professionals. We hope that the debate will continue.

For anyone located within design, visual studies' failure to acknowledge and address the central role of graphic design as a shaper of the visual environment, alongside the forms of visual culture that it does acknowledge — art, film, television, photography, advertising, new media — must seem unaccountable. What could explain this peculiar blindness among a group of academics hyper-attuned to most forms of visuality?

Rick Poynor

Out of the Studio: Graphic Design History and Visual Studies – Design Observer (2011)

1. Why and How?

The role of research in graphic design: semiotics, analysis, communication theory, systematic approaches, semantics and discourse theory

Research Methodologies

This book is intended to provide an introduction into the area of research methodologies for graphic designers. This important aspect of graphic design practice encompasses a wide range of practical and theoretical applications and this chapter introduces the field of research methodology as both an analytical and a practical tool for graphic designers.

By investigating these twin areas of research in parallel, we aim to establish the role of critical thinking as a support to the development of what can be described as an engaged form of design practice. Research is an intrinsic aspect of design practice and an essential part of the activity of problem solving. The designer is involved in a constant process of enquiry. It could be said that this process is predicated upon the notion of questioning – whether that leads to a discrete outcome or solution, such as an industrial prototype based on a client's needs, or whether it contributes to the discourse and debate in the form of a proposition or a further question.

Primary theoretical models of design analysis and visual research will also be introduced, including semiotics, communication theory, systematic approaches to design problem solving, semantics, rhetoric and discourse theory as well as secondary research models and the testing of ideas and methodologies. The underlying emphasis throughout this book is on why we do what we do and how, through testing, feedback and rigorous approaches, we can be sure it is effective in the process of visual communication.

Methodology
The science of method, or a body of methods, employed in a particular activity such as the research aspects of a project. A logical, predefined, and systematic strategy by which to undertake and progress a graphic design project, to include methods of evaluation of experimental outcomes, a schedule for each stage of the project and a stated intention or purpose in relation to a range of anticipated outcomes.

It could also be employed to describe an approach to graphic design in general: a particular manner of working or a procedure used in the production of graphic design. Sometimes used in reference to organization or a technique of organizing and analysing, or a scheme of classification.

Method
A way of proceeding or doing something, especially in a systematic or regular manner – an action or system of actions toward a goal.

Problematizing Design

The discipline of graphic design can be defined in a variety of ways – the most persistent definition over its relatively short history has described the role of visual communication as a problem-solving activity. This phrase, something of a mantra for a large section of the design community, has been employed to describe the function of graphic design in a commercial sense – a sound bite that can be understood by the commissioners of designers – the clients.

This definition has not only legitimized the business and commercial aspects of design, but in parallel has led to a restricted description of the function of graphic design that often excludes what might be considered as the wider social, educational and informational roles of the profession. A broader interpretation of the term 'problem solving' could characterize it as a process of analysis and synthesis.

Analysis relates to the methods of investigation, enquiry and understanding central to the research of a project brief, concept or a particular context. Synthesis, meanwhile, is the means by which a designer is able to draw upon his or her initial analytical work and investigation to produce meaningful solutions or interventions. This ability is based upon the individual designer's intentions and their understanding of a complex range of interrelated issues affecting the creation of a successful graphic solution: audience, message or product, budget, materials, the means of production, the use of an appropriate visual language and the final form the outcome will take.

Communication Theory
The body of work that relates to the study of communication and the ways in which meaning is transferred between individuals and groups through language or media.

Semiotics
The study of signs and symbols, especially the relationship between written or spoken signs and their referents in the physical world or the world of ideas. Semiotic theory can be seen as a core strategic method by which graphic marks, texts and images can be deconstructed and interpreted to determine their underlying meanings.

Semantics
The branch of linguistics that deals with the study of meaning. The study of the relationships between signs and symbols and the meaning that they represent.

Rhetoric
The study of the technique of the effective use of language. Written or spoken discourse used to persuade, influence or affect an audience.

Discourse
A body of verbal or written communication, especially between two or more participants. The act of discussion between parties, often in a formal manner.

Linguistics
The scientific study of language and its underlying structure.

Research Methodologies

Terms of Reference

Many strategies can be applied to this basic framework for research in graphic design, and a number of these methodologies bring with them specific terms that are useful to the designer in describing what is taking place in the development and staging of a graphic design project. A significant proportion of these terms are drawn from outside the field of graphic design and are borrowed from allied or tangential disciplines that have a long tradition of reflection and debate. Subjects such as linguistics, communication studies, philosophy and the social sciences, for example, have provided useful terms and definitions that designers have been able to adapt and employ in the foundation of a more descriptive language for the processes at work within the creation of visual solutions.

This is not to suggest that graphic design lacks its own specific language. Like many activities with a background and history in the technological arena, designers have developed a wide range of terms to describe what is at work in the production of visual communication. A large proportion of this terminology is rooted in the pragmatic description of technical issues, such as colour and type specification and printing processes, or is influenced by the now commonplace computer and software language.

The designer and historian Richard Hollis has described graphic design as constituting a language in its own right, '...*a language with an uncertain grammar and a continuously expanding vocabulary.*' At the same time, terms from outside the discipline have also been utilized to describe a wider, less technically orientated approach to graphic design: theoretical terms such as 'gestalt' or 'rhetoric' (see pages 72–73) often appear in the general discussion of graphic design or in relation to an individual designer's

Epistemology
The theory of the underlying methods or grounds of knowledge, and the critical study of the validity, methods and scope of an established body of knowledge. In relation to graphic design, this indicates the body of widely accepted knowledge that defines the discipline, including those theories surrounding legibility, written language and typography, as well as those drawn from outside of the profession.

Theories such as gestalt, for example, have been drawn from the discipline of psychology and employed by designers in their working methods and practices. These ideas have influenced the everyday discussion of graphic design practice and the language used by designers to explain their working methods.

Gestalt
Drawn from a branch of psychology that deals with the human mind and behaviour in relation to perception, Gestalt theory can be understood as being based upon the whole being greater than the sum of the individual parts.

Within graphic design, this theory can be applied to visual organisation and composition based on the understanding that human beings tend to perceive groups or groupings in two ways: as being unified/similar or different/varied.

The knowledge that elements on a page for example can be visually organised to direct the viewer or user toward certain readings or understandings is central to the activity of visual communication.

approach to a project. This expanding vocabulary partly refers to the relationship between graphic design and technology – a relationship that has defined the subject during its historical development.

The most recent, and probably the most significant, development for contemporary graphic designers has been the arrival of the Apple Macintosh computer (introduced in 1984), bringing with it a new language related to design. At the same time, this advance has made obsolete many of the traditional processes and terms used by graphic designers, which related to an earlier age of mechanical, rather than electronic, reproduction. The debate surrounding the impact and value of this particular technology continues today, more than 25 years after its initial introduction. The Macintosh has indisputably altered the landscape of graphic design, allowing designers to function in a way not previously possible and offering new creative opportunities with greater levels of control over production processes. As a work platform the computer has been influential in opening up new opportunities for designers, while also acting as a catalyst for much of the new debate within the profession, which could be termed a design discourse. The many discussions, for instance those surrounding notions of authorship, audience and legibility, exemplified in journals such as *Eye Magazine* and *Emigre* in the early 21st century, have encouraged designers to explore new roles in what Dutch designer and educator Jan van Toorn has described as '…*the designer's field of operation'*.

There can be a discipline of design, but it must be different in kind from disciplines which possess determinate subject matters. Design is a discipline where the conception of subject matter, method, and purpose is an integrated part of the activity and of the results… not products, as such, but the art of conceiving and planning products.

Richard Buchanan
'Rhetoric, Humanism and Design' in *Discovering Design: Explorations in Design Studies* (1995)

Process and Product

The South American design educator and writer Jorge Frascara has written that '…*the design of the design method and the design of the research method are tasks of a higher order than the design of the communications.*' This statement identifies a key shift in design thinking in recent years. The expanding definition of what might be considered the practice of graphic design has been influenced by factors other than technology. The speculative and more experimental work at the margins of contemporary graphic design, an area which could be termed the 'avant-garde', together with a range of self-authored graphic projects produced by designers working to their own brief, has also exerted a strong influence.

These initiatives often offer new visual grammars and graphic forms, and can focus on areas of graphic design previously constrained and under-examined by a singular, commercially focused definition of the discipline. This recent concentration upon the processes and methods involved in graphic design – a conscious reflection on the *how* and the *why* of the practice, has allowed the area of research methodologies to take on a greater degree of significance to the subject.

The discussion of graphic design in university design departments, art colleges and design journals now routinely includes reference to a diverse set of issues that include the designer's responsibilities in a social, cultural and economic sense, the role of the designer in communicating to audiences and the construction of meaning in verbal and visual languages. This wider field of operation has increased the exploration of the processes at work and has broadened the scope of research in graphic design, both within the academies and the professional arena.

Primary Research
The raw materials that a designer directly works with in relation to research. Primary research approaches might include marketing strategies, such as audience surveys or interviews, or the direct testing of potential visual solutions within a 'real world' context.

Secondary Research
Established or existing research already undertaken in the field and used to support the designer's own research. This might include published surveys and/or interviews with potential audience groups, together with the analysis of a range of successful visual communication strategies within a similar context.

Tertiary Research
Research based on secondary sources and the research of others synthesized to simply restate what others have undertaken. A summary of the existing body of knowledge and accepted methodologies relating to the range of intentions, audience and context of the project.

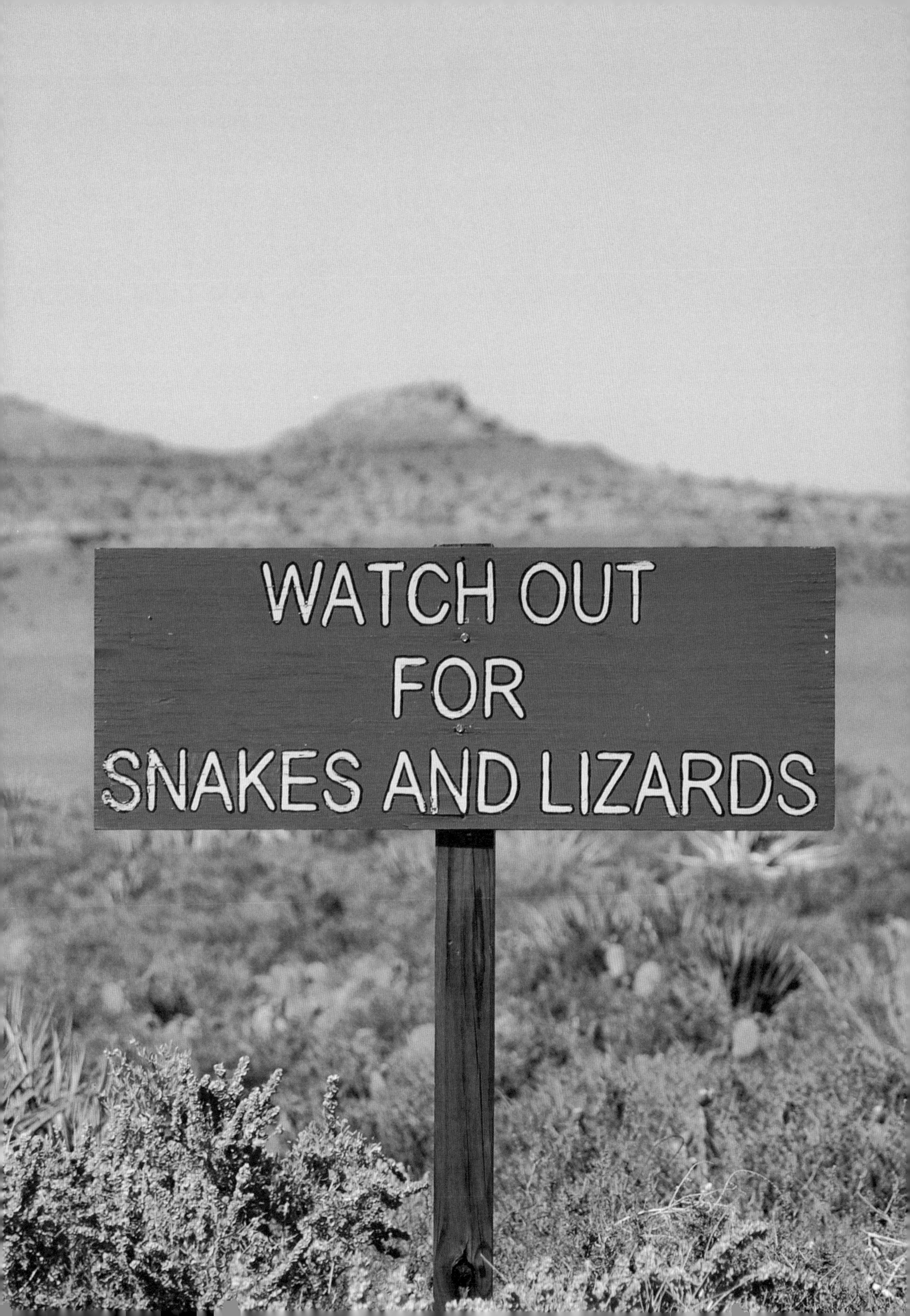
WATCH OUT
FOR
SNAKES AND LIZARDS

Design Commentators

For a long period during the development of the discipline the discussion of graphic design as an activity and its place in the wider community was left to external voices – those who received or observed design, rather than those who created it. Whilst this provided in itself a useful tool for understanding graphic design, very few of these voices were heard from within the practice itself.

Journalists, historians and cultural theorists who have written about graphic design have usually done so in terms of the artefact or end product and its effect in a social or cultural context. With very few exceptions, the process of design problem solving, the methodologies employed by designers and their intentions and conceptual approaches to the *practice* of graphic design were left under-explored in print and in the general discussion of the subject. Meanwhile, commentary from within the profession was long

centred on commercial portfolio reviews, award-winning designs and designers, and the tools of the trade, from the Rotring pen to the Apple Macintosh.

As the emphasis has moved away from the external commentator on design, it has instead become increasingly centred upon the growing community of designers and educators who are motivated by the idea of what has been termed the 'reflective practitioner'– the notion of designers commenting on their own practice. Designers are now regular contributors to journals and speakers at lectures and conferences. We have witnessed an avalanche of graphic design publications, all with varying degrees of insight, which focus on the processes and intentions at work. Educational programmes and practitioners are beginning to build upon this graphic design discourse and are, in the process, expanding the definition of graphic design practice itself.

Avant-garde

From the French term meaning literally the vanguard or front-runner. In the context of art and design, the term avant-garde is usually employed to describe the pioneers or innovators of a particular period or movement, often in opposition to the mainstream or status quo.

Both avant-garde and vanguard were created by combining the old French words *avant*, meaning 'fore', and

garde, meaning 'guard' and relate to its original usage by the military.

The notion of the vanguard could also be considered to be a heterodoxy – meaning different, contrary to or unorthodox (in fact, the term heterodox, rather than unorthodox, is the antonym of orthodox).

In graphic design the term avant-garde is rarely used in the discussion

of contemporary design activity – more often than not the phrase is applied when discussing the history of the subject. This is not to suggest that there is no current avant-garde in graphic design, simply that the phrase has passed out of common usage.

Interestingly, the relationship between the mainstream and the avant-garde operates in a very particular fashion. There are a

number of celebrated designers around the world who are considered 'cutting edge' and radical in their approach to design whilst maintaining a successful commercial career with mainstream clients.

For example, designers such as Stefan Sagmeister and David Carson have received critical acclaim for their ground-breaking and influential work, but have also attracted big corporate clients – in the case of

Research and Development

This shift towards an engaged and reflective practice is not in direct conflict with the traditions of commercial facilitation. Instead, the mutuality or interdependence between design experimentation and investigation and applied design thinking in a commercial sense is increased – allowing ideas of effectiveness and usefulness to inform original and propositional approaches equally.

As Ronald Barnett discusses in his book *Higher Education: A Critical Business* (1997): '...*the essential idea in this tradition in the Western university is that it is possible to critique action so as to produce more enlightened or more effective forms of action. The critical thinking in this tradition is a practice in the world, a praxis. Knowledge situated in practice is not, as is sometimes implied, a newish form of knowing alongside propositional knowledge, but is a tradition of enduring character.'* Reflection on practice can, then, lead to more informed judgements, the refinement of tools and techniques, and a better defined methodological framework, both for the core subject of graphic design as an academic discipline and the wider graphic design profession.

Carson, working later in his career with companies such as Microsoft.

This interdependency between the radical and propositional visual grammars of new and challenging work and the mainstream of design can be described as a process of recoupment. This phrase was coined by the situationists during the late 1960s to describe the ability of mainstream culture to accommodate 'outsider' ideas. The current situation is more symbiotic than the phrase recoupment suggests. The large fees paid by corporate clients support the time and space to allow designers to explore and experiment.

In turn the new ideas and visual styles that emerge from this feed into the mainstream of the discipline and become influential for a new generation of emerging designers.

Key Concepts: The Designer as Author

A significant shift in the range of approaches to contemporary graphic design has come about as a result of the debate surrounding the notion of **graphic authorship** and what this might constitute in the future for graphic designers. While definitions of authorship in graphic design continue to be expanded and updated by designers, design writers and educators, it is useful to consider a singular interpretation as a starting point for further debate.

Traditionally, graphic designers are involved in a process of facilitation: put concisely, the business of design is to communicate other people's messages to specified audiences – to respond to a brief that has been originated and defined by a client. This might be for the purposes of providing general information (such as a train timetable or road sign) or to persuade a target audience about a particular product through its packaging and promotional design. While this may be a crude definition, it is clearly applicable to the broad majority of design practices in the commercial arena: graphic designers are commissioned to employ their skills as communicators in the service of a client.

The notion of **authorship** lies in the possibility that designers can also operate as mediators – that they can take responsibility for the **content** and **context** of a message as well as the more traditional means of communication.

The focus for the designer might be on the transmission of their own ideas and messages, without the need for a client or commissioner, but sill remaining fixed on the effectiveness of communicating with an audience. It might also arise from an exploration into an area of personal interest, or the observation of a 'real world' problem that the designer feels could be better addressed. The designer might establish an operational solution as a pitch to sell to potential sponsors or clients, in the same way that an inventor or product designer may create original products and models through which to present a business case to potential investors.

Graphic authorship can also operate in a commercial sense – a client might choose to employ a graphic designer because they have a particular visual style or method of working that would work in tandem with their message or product. This could be described a designer's signature style, and there are many celebrated or well-known designers who are commissioned purely because of a body of work that is concerned with particular themes or is popular with a particular audience.

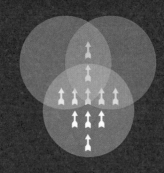

AUTHOR
DESIGNER
READER

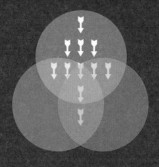

2. Design Literacy

Research through making, iterative approaches to graphic design, problem finding and problem solving

Visual Literacy in Design Practice

Design literacy, or visual literacy in design practice, is a fundamental concern for those involved in the creation of visual communication. The understanding of the interrelationship between formal considerations of shape, colour, organization and composition and the cultural signposts embedded in graphic communication is at the heart of successful and effective approaches to design. Whilst it is difficult to point to a considerable body of knowledge that might constitute an epistemology of graphic design, in particular theories and ideas which directly relate to the act of designing, it is reasonable to accept that many of the formal aspects of design are informed by a wide range of underpinning ideas and theories.

Principles such as gestalt – meaning unified whole, and drawn from psychology and the understanding of how human visual perception behaves – are at the heart of graphic design. The ways in which visual elements that make up a design are able to communicate in a more or less effective fashion are largely dependent on a range of factors that are described by some of the defining principles of gestalt and perception.

The fundamental principle or law of gestalt is known as Prägnanz, and is based on the human tendency to organize in a manner that is regular, symmetrical and to a large degree based on simplicity. The theory of the innate laws by which objects and their relationships can be perceived as organized or grouped is a useful building block for the designer in understanding how composition can communicate meaning to a viewer or user.

This analysis of form and of relationships within a composition is informed by thinking about design in terms of concepts such as: closure, similarity, proximity, symmetry and continuity (see page 29).

Form
The shape or configuration of something, as against its location, context or meaning. This could also indicate the pattern or structure of an object or image. In graphic design, this relates to the physical nature of the designed artefact, rather than the intention of the design or designer or any inherent message or communication.

Function
The performance or role played by an object or form. The service performed by a work of graphic design or visual communication. The classic phrase 'form follows function' relates to the manner in which modernist architects and designers attempted to shape outcomes in relation to the problem being addressed, rather than taking a stylistically led approach to design.

Context
The circumstances that are relevant to an event or situation. In graphic design terms, this would indicate a clear description of the purpose or intention of a brief alongside secondary research into similar propositions or situations – historical or contemporary – together with audience expectations, the visual environment and the background to the brief itself.

Concept
A hypothesis, theory or idea. The fundamental aspects of the brief and the intention of the designer. In formal terms, a concept also suggests a methodology or plan of action through which to test or pursue the idea.

These ideas, drawn from a branch of psychology that has its basis in the holistic, can be described in general as the whole being greater than the sum of its parts.

Ways of Thinking

Max Wertheimer, one of the central and founding figures of gestalt psychology, also describes how thinking can be considered in two ways: productive thinking and reproductive thinking. The former is based upon problem solving and its relationship to the notion of insight: unplanned and immediate responses to situations and environments. The second mode, reproductive thinking, is based upon what has previously been learned and understood. These ideas relate to a more considered approach to visual communication and the processes at work in the creation of a design, and to those factors at work in systems of communication.

Invisible Systems

There are a number of other significant ideas that can be drawn from outside of design and that could also be considered as useful in describing the basis of a rigorous approach to visual/design literacy. These can be broken down into ideas concerned with composition, colour, materials and form.

The grid or system at work 'beneath' a design – a structure created to ensure harmony and consistency within the layout of a book or poster – can be thought about using ideas related to the golden ratio. This is also known as the 'golden section' or the 'golden mean'. This ratio can be found at work in nature, art and architecture and can be described mathematically by dividing a line into two parts so that the longer part divided by the shorter part is equal to the whole length divided by the longer part.

In English the word 'design' is both a noun and a verb. As a noun, it means – among other things – intention, plan, intent, aim, scheme, plot, motif, basic structure, all these being connected with cunning and deception. As a verb – to design – meanings include to concoct something, to simulate, to draft, to sketch, to fashion, to have designs on something.

Vilém Flusser
The Shape of Things: A Philosophy of Design (1999)

Visual Literacy in Design Practice

It is argued that this ratio is generally found to create a fundamental aesthetic preference in the majority of individuals. Like a number of these 'rules' or 'laws' its value is not in providing a strict code or doctrine of operation for designers, but in providing a rationale or explanation – a tool and a guide for understanding. The golden section has a strong relationship to the Fibonacci number sequence – a similar system, in this case based on number relationships in a linear sequence: each number being the sum of the previous two numbers; 0, 1, 1, 2, 3, 5, 8, 13, 21, 34, 55, 89 and so on. This model can be applied to grid systems and even the relationship between type size and leading in text setting for editorial layouts.

Composition and editing can be considered using a technique known as the 'rule of thirds'. This again has a strong relation to the golden section and is based upon dividing a given area into thirds both vertically and horizontally to create a grid structure of nine rectangles that have four intersections. This knowledge can be useful when constructing a layout.

Material Ideas

The understanding of the relationship between the materials employed in a design and the message that is 'given off' is a significant factor that can be explained by the theory of affordances (see pages 182–183). This theory relates to the physical properties employed in a design – it's 'materiality'. For example, the format and cover of a book creates an effect or emotional response in the user whether through the choice of materials employed, the shape and scale of the book or the use of illustration or photography. Whilst the photograph or reproduction does not itself afford anything, it triggers an association with the affordance of the object in the mind of the viewer.

Generative Systems

Generative systems are employed by the designer in the process of form making. The phrase, drawn from tangential design disciplines, such as architecture and engineering, is intended to encompass design activities that have a direct influence on the form of what is produced.

The study or use of generative systems as part of a working design research methodology involves an understanding of the explicit relationship between the systematic aspects of a project (the process, considerations and decision-making processes) and the final visual form or product (its properties, composition and performance).

01 Principles of Gestalt >>
The organization of a whole that is more than the sum of its parts. The implication of meaning communicated through the use of a part of an image or object, rather than the whole.

Similarity

Continuity

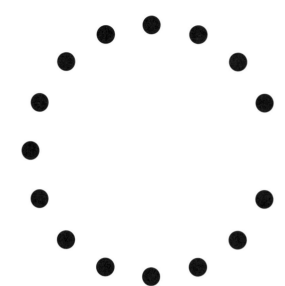

Closure

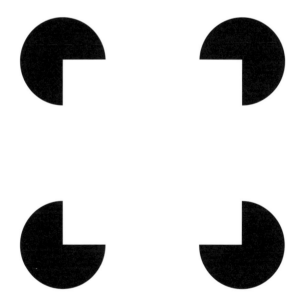

Proximity

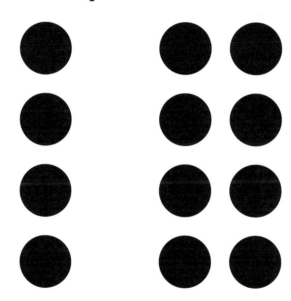

Similarity

This principle states that objects that share similar visual characteristics; shape, size, colour and so on, create a connection in the viewer's mind implying that they are related or naturally belong together. In the diagram above horizontal lines of the same sized shape appear to be grouped together because alternately they are either solids or outline.

Closure

In this example the effect is created in the mind of a white square floating above four solid circles, even though there is no square. The principle of closure states that when elements are aligned in such a way that we perceive that the information is connected, we tend to see complete figures even when some of the information is missing.

Continuity

The gestalt principle at work here is that closure occurs when an object is incomplete or a space is not entirely enclosed. Provided enough of the shape is indicated, we perceive the object as whole by filling in the information that is absent, thus completing the circle.

Proximity

Proximity occurs when objects or elements are placed close together. They tend to be perceived as a group or a unified whole. In the example above, the vertical lines of dots that are closer together appear to be more related to each other or are understood as a single unit, separate from the single line of dots on the left.

Visual Literacy in Design Practice

Visual Meaning

Other significant areas of design literacy involve the consideration of how colour is used within an overall composition. Whilst the intelligent selection of colour palettes and combinations of colours can be employed to a create design that is aesthetically pleasing to the viewer, it can also work to emphasize hierarchies, structures and relationships. These uses of colour are directly related to formal composition within graphic design, but there is also a more complex consideration that requires another form of visual literacy on the part of the designer. This is in the area of cultural association and how messages are encoded and decoded by particular audiences dependent on issues such as background, education and age, for example.

In many parts of the world, colour is used to indicate meaning when associated with shape. Road traffic sign systems provide a good example of this.

In the UK a traffic sign that has a red border and a triangular shape is understood to mean a warning. Whilst there is some basis in our innate natural physical response to colours such as red – it raises blood pressure and respiration – our reactions to that colour in that particular context are based on cultural preconceptions. Recognizing the triangular form of the road sign can be thought of as a learned behaviour. It implies a reaction shaped through experience and social convention; it is agreed to represent a warning and is implicitly an instruction we are conditioned to observe and react to.

This has wider connotations for the designer who is required to create attractive and discriminable visual communication but also who, in order to be effective, is required to construct messages that can be widely understood. This is dependent on the individual designer's empathy and knowledge of the

---

Text

The use of the word 'text' refers to more than the printed word on a page in a book. It also encompasses a number of other activities and items related to cultural production, such as the wide range of visual and aural forms of communication. This would include, for example, a film, a wrestling match on television or a building – anything that carries meaning and that could be 'read' by an audience.

In the late 1960s and early 1970s the French philosopher Roland Barthes began to challenge the existing idea that the author of a book could be considered as the central and controlling influence on the meaning of a text.

In his essays 'The Death of the Author' and 'From Work to Text', Barthes argues that while it is possible to trace the influence of the author in a text, the text itself

remains 'open', encouraging the idea that the meaning is brought to an object – particularly a cultural object – by its intended audience. In this way, the meaning does not intrinsically reside in the object itself and cannot be reduced to an authorial intention.

Barthes related 'the death of the author' with 'the birth of the reader', claiming that *a text's unity lies not in its origin but in its destination*.

audience they are attempting to talk to. An awareness of how the individual components that comprise a designed message will be understood or specifically interpreted is a central concern to ensure that what is meant is what is communicated.

As technologies allow us to become more and more interconnected, the manner in which we communicate has an increasingly global context. This places a further demand on the visual communicator to understand the significance of many of the smaller elements of a design. Shape and colour, for example, and how they are understood, are not based upon universal conventions and are open to interpretation. The study of this is known as semiotics (see pages 92–93) and also relates to areas such as image and text. Semiotics or semiology can be thought of as the science of signs and how they operate in the world. It can also be understood in terms of connotation and denotation: the relationship between the literal or primary meaning of something and its secondary interpreted meaning (see pages 46–47).

It would be easy to think of visual literacy in design as something only concerned with the formal aspects of composition, but for a design to work effectively a wider set of cultural considerations have to be understood to ensure that the process of interpretation and denotation are equally built into an overall approach to visual communication. These understandings provide the foundations from which effective design is created.

Complex social problems do not get solved by just doing things; things have to be done well. This requires effort, intelligence, cultural and ethical sensitivity, resources and institutional support. The design response to a social problem cannot be conceived as the production of a few posters and flyers that tell people what to do and what not to do.

Jorge Frascara
User-Centred Graphic Design: Mass Communications and Social Change (1997)

Case Study 01: **Visual Grammar**

The following three case studies explore how individual designers have approached the area of visual grammar within their own personal projects. Charlotte Knibbs explores the form of the square in two and three dimensions. Her work (pages 33–35) plays with the movement of the square through planes and angles in two dimensions to create motion and tension through what might be termed optical illusion. This series of experiments is repeated in three dimensions using photography to recreate her earlier experiments; employing lighting, perspective and angle or aspect of view to create optical effects and communicate with the viewer.

Niall O'Shea's work (pages 36–39) began with an investigation into the circle and dot and progressively grew to encompass an exploration of photo-mechanical reproduction and in particular the half-tone process. This exhaustive study involved a wide range of subtle and gradual changes in the scale and arrangement of key elements such as the dot and the line to create more or less detail in images and to generate patterns.

There is a strong link between these two projects and the work of Edouard Pecher (see pages 40–45), which is concerned with visual grammar and generative systems and in particular the creation of a system of visual oppositions. These explorations are concerned with a detailed investigation of how form is related to key aspects of communication, such as meaning and perception. The ability to understand and control these key factors is essential in the design of effective visual communication. These projects are also linked by process and a focus on the iterative nature of design research: the slow and methodical testing of an idea and the identification of potential opportunities arising from that research.

Charlotte Knibbs: Planar Square
Knibbs initially set out to explore the square, starting with some varied visual experiments to test everything she thought she knew about the form, its geometry and its appearance. She began by altering the dimensions of the square as a simple four-sided figure, its angles and sides, and created an extensive visual audit of the changes she observed during the experiments.

The most notable of these graphic images showed how, when apparently warped and twisted, the shape of the square can be used to create many other varied shapes and optical illusions, in particular the impression of a two-dimensional form rotating and moving sequentially relative to an implied plane (opposite page).

Following these experiments in altering flat two-dimensional images of the square by skewing the original shape – creating rhombus, parallelograms, and diamonds – Knibbs decided to extend the experiment into three-dimensional space, charting the changes to a 'fixed' square through observation in perspective. She created a series of photographic exercises that attempted to mimic the same distorted shapes of her two-dimensional geometric planes by varying the angle and distance of the lens (the viewer) to the square object mounted on a wall.

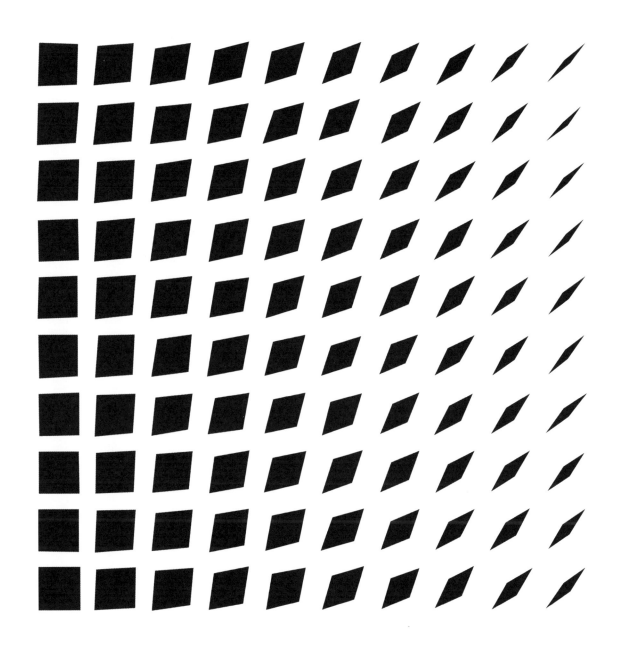

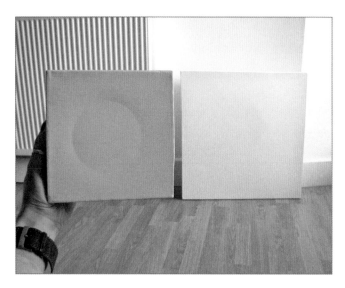

Depth and Perspective

Following her experiments into 2D and 3D squares, Knibbs moved on to the three-dimensional square form, the cube. Working with a group of fellow design students, she began to make simple investigations into the form of the cube and its relationship to light and perspective. They observed that shining a light at 90° to the square would always form long rectangular shadows that stretched across the surface that the square was placed upon. Any changes to the angle of the light, the object, or the viewer, and the shape of the shadow created would completely change (opposite page).

Knibbs then experimented with depth of field and diminution – a term that simply describes how shapes or objects further away will seem smaller in comparison to those closer to the viewer. She created two square canvases of completely different sizes and placed them in parallel but not on the same plane. Because the larger of the two squares was placed in the distance it can be made to appear the same size as the smaller square (top left), or relatively scaled to it in varying degrees (top right and above).

While these experiments are extremely simple, each informed Knibbs' further development on the project. Her final resolution employed a range of practical techniques developed during this phase of her research process to build a three-dimensional typographic installation that could be read from only one perspective viewpoint.

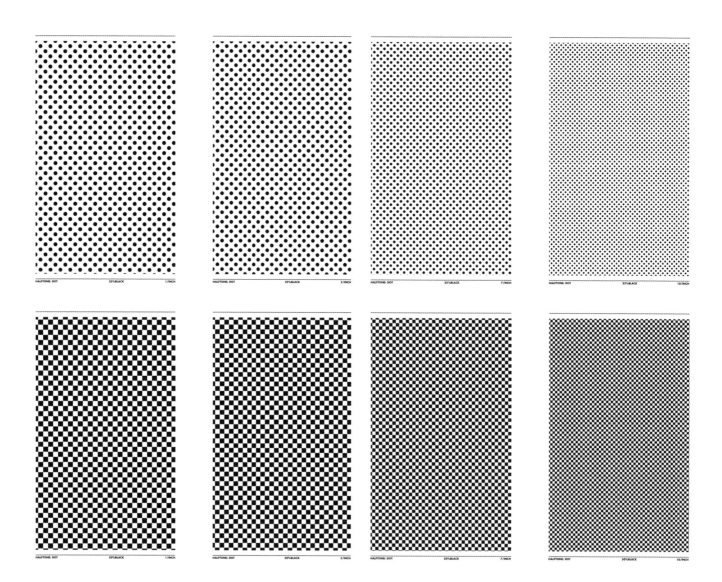

Niall O'Shea: Half-tone

The term half-tone is used to describe a reprographic printing technique that commonly produces a simulation of continuous tone imagery through the use of dots or lines, varying either in size or in spacing. While continuous tone imagery might contain an infinite range of colours or greys, the half-tone process reduces visual reproductions to a binary image that is printed with only one colour of ink in terms of black and white imagery, or four process colours for 'full colour' visualization. This binary reproduction relies on a basic optical illusion – the fact that these tiny variations in tone are blended into smooth gradients and colours by the human eye.

O'Shea initially set out to explore the basic form and context of the circle, before moving on to the concept of the dot, and ultimately the visual patterns created in the production of half-tone images. Part of his working process involved the exhaustive documentation of a range of half-tone patterns and screens that were designed for image reproduction at different levels of detail and resolution (above and opposite).

These screens were traditionally used as film overlays on continuous tone images (such as illustrations or high resolution photographs) in the production of printing plates. Variations in pattern include both round and square dots and lines of different size and thickness.

HALFTONE: LINE   25%.BLACK   1/INCH
HALFTONE: LINE   25%.BLACK   5/INCH
HALFTONE: LINE   25%.BLACK   7/INCH
HALFTONE: LINE   25%.BLACK   10/INCH

HALFTONE: LINE   50%.BLACK   1/INCH
HALFTONE: LINE   50%.BLACK   5/INCH
HALFTONE: LINE   50%.BLACK   7/INCH
HALFTONE: LINE   50%.BLACK   10/INCH

HALFTONE: LINE   75%.BLACK   7/INCH
HALFTONE: LINE   75%.BLACK   10/INCH
HALFTONE: LINE   75%.BLACK   15/INCH
HALFTONE: LINE   75%.BLACK   30/INCH

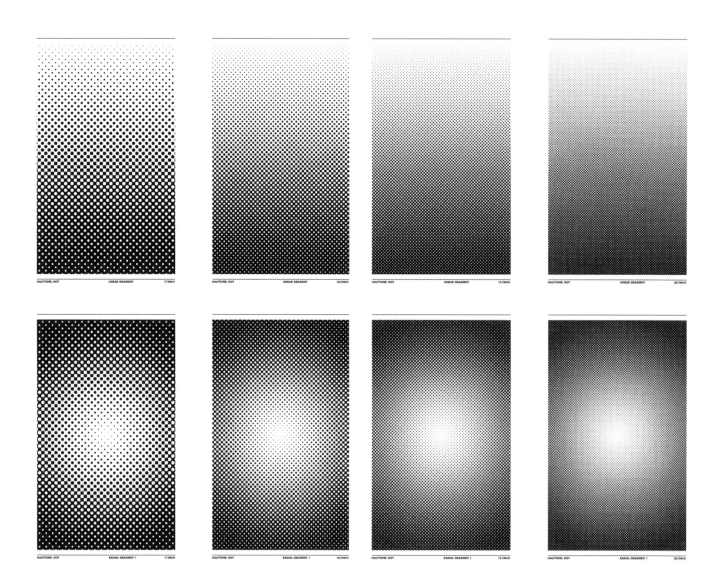

Contrasting Images

Digital print processes have been steadily replacing photographic half-toning since the late 1970s, and this process has developed more rapidly since the advent of desktop publishing and a more integrated approach to digital graphic design from origination to final output. Initially, electronic dot generators were developed for the film recorder units linked to colour drum scanners, and more recently direct-to-plate digital printing has utilized stochastic patterns based on more scattered and less regular dots and lines in order to produce an impression of higher resolution and more natural images.

O'Shea continued to apply his half-tone pattern analysis to the variation of dot size and line thickness in the reproduction of a range of gradients and special effects (above) and images (opposite top). Variations in dot and line clearly demonstrate the ways in which more or less detail might be revealed, though this needs to be balanced against the ability of the printing press and print stock to 'hold' smaller dots cleanly and clearly.

Finally, O'Shea applied the same process to typography (opposite bottom). This is an area not normally subject to the half-tone process, since type is usually reproduced in a solid colour, such as black ink on a white background.

HALFTONE: DOT   IMAGE   15/INCH

HALFTONE: DOT   IMAGE   20/INCH

HALFTONE: DOT   25%BLACK   7/INCH

HALFTONE: DOT   25%BLACK   10/INCH

HALFTONE: LINE   25%BLACK   7/INCH

HALFTONE: LINE   25%BLACK   10/INCH

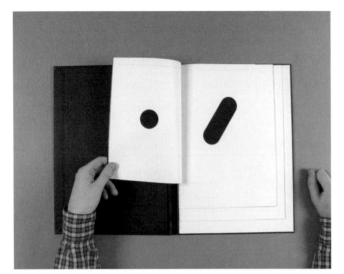

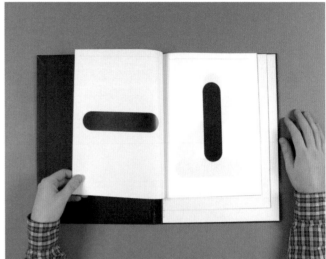

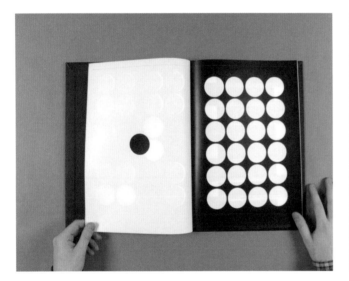

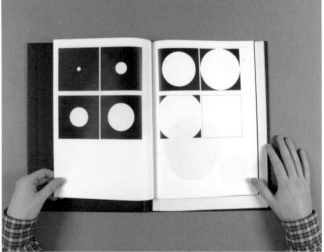

Edouard Pecher: A System of Oppositions

In these extracts from his initial research project, Edouard Pecher explores the relationship between fundamental forms such as circles, squares and triangles. In particular his investigation builds upon how these forms can work in opposition to each other to establish contrast and create meaning. Using basic elements such as the dot and the line, the project explores how to create direction, movement, tone, texture and scale. Much of the work pictured here was undertaken to build an understanding of visual grammar and to discover how this can inform a general approach to graphic design.

The acceptance that the majority of visual communication is based upon the basic building blocks of these visual forms and their relationship to each other is not a singular and formal way of thinking about design but is more based in the understanding of the connection between the visual and the conceptual.

These underlying principles of form and design are informed by key ideas such as gestalt theory (see pages 28–29) and the writings of Dondis A. Dondis, Rudolf Arnheim, Wucius Wong, Christian Leborg and Gyorgy Kepes.

The visual elements employed are described by Pecher as a 'kit of parts' – the elements of a personal visual language through which he can begin to construct meaning for the viewer. This process of building an idiosyncratic visual language became focused on the development of what Pecher titles 'a system of oppositions'. This subsequently led to a secondary and more applied project that can be seen on pages 42–45.

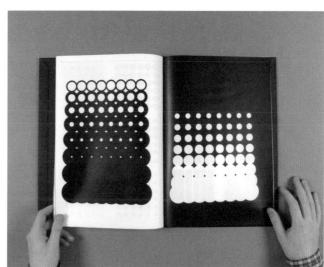

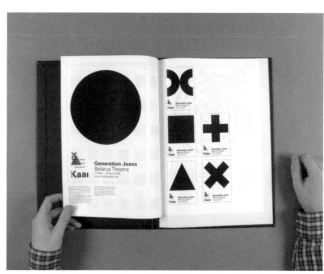

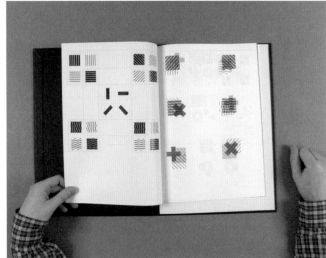

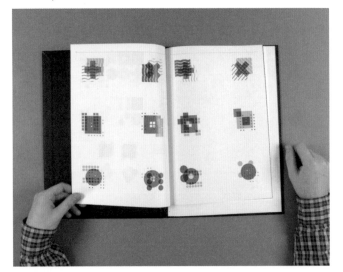

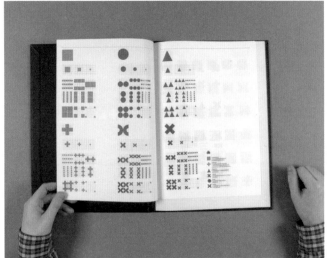

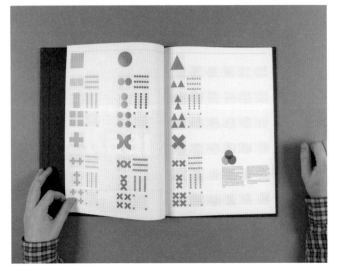

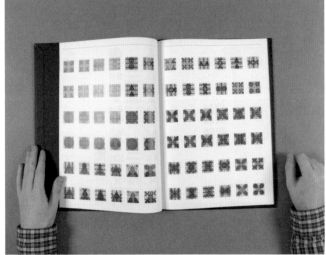

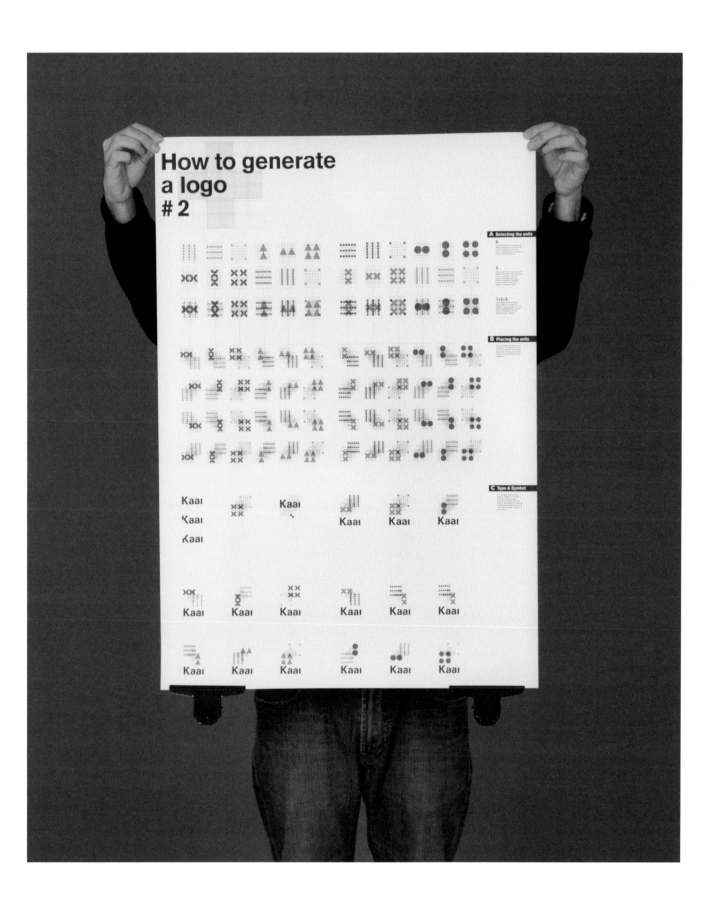

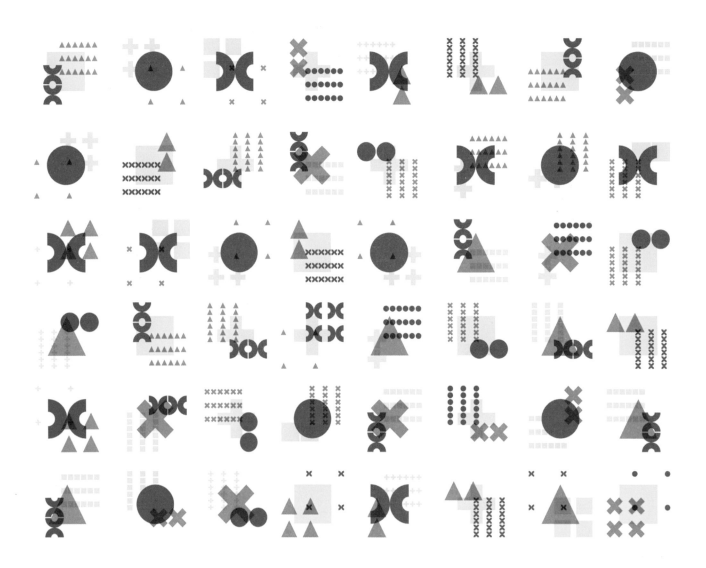

The System Maintains

This branding project builds upon the earlier work and the notion of visual oppositions to create a generative system for the graphic identity of a theatre in Belgium. Generativity in this context relies on an algorithm or formula created by Pecher to produce a large number of permutations and relationships between shapes and colours. These rules allow him to create an identity that is not fixed in the way a traditional logotype would behave, across a range of print and screen-based applications. The system relies on the 'rules' created by Pecher to create an identity that defines itself. There is a fundamental relationship between the system and the theatre: the theatre is based in a city and country where two languages are spoken and is also based on two locations on a north/south axis to each other.

To create the system, Pecher created defining rules based upon contrasting elements of squares, triangles and circles, colours and lines.. These elements are organized within an overall square shape. By using this delineated palette he is able to create a visual system of a vast range of combinations and permutations and also develop a homogeneous and visually consistent feel to the identity.

The final outcome to the project is not an endless number of variations created by the designer himself. Pecher chose instead to refocus on how the system itself could become the basis of the identity, and how he could communicate the design of the system to other designers who could then apply the rules he had created for themselves when working on design material for the theatre.

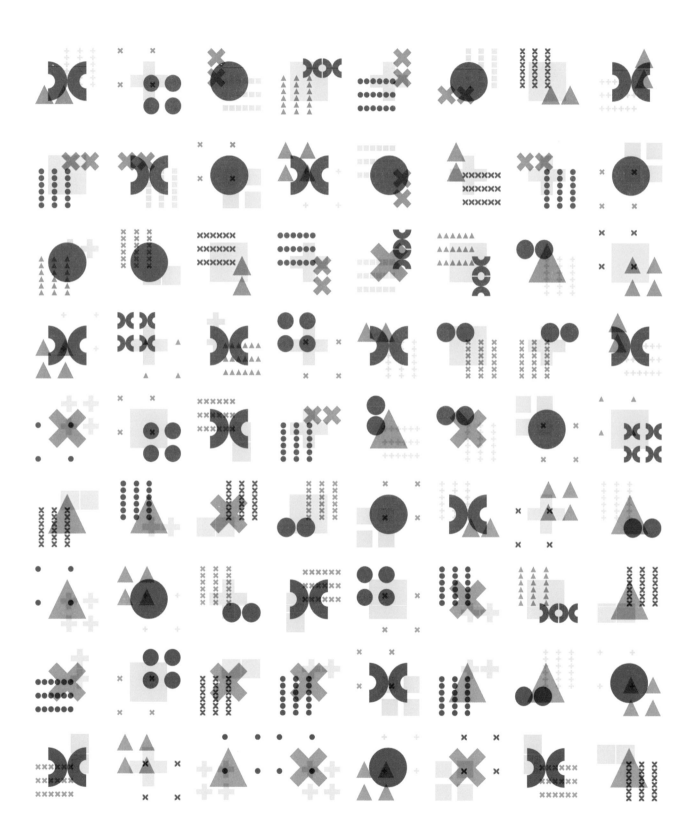

Key Concepts: Connotation and Denotation

The term **denotation** is used to describe the primary, literal meaning of an image or a piece of communication, usually in relation to a particular target audience or group of readers. Like a name or noun, it describes what an object is, in and of itself, rather than what it means. This aspect of reading (decoding) and writing or making (encoding) meaning within a message is fundamental to all forms of communication.

Graphic designers need to be aware of the uses of particular visual signs and symbols, and their common meanings, within a target group. This is especially true within fields such as information design and the other areas of graphic design that attempt to reach a broad audience, and therefore rely heavily on the denotation of specific meanings within visual forms in order to make the intended message clear. The context within which the message is to be read is crucial here, as are the specific material qualities of the visual form itself: for instance it may be handwritten, typeset, drawn, photographed, printed or on screen, each of which will affect the ways in which the message is interpreted.

Connotation refers to the range of secondary meanings, either intended or unintended, within a form of communication (such as a text; written, verbal or visual): the range of meanings and interpretations of an object or thing, its qualities and impressions in the eyes of the reader. The meaning of the image and how we 'read' it is not fixed by its creator or author but is equally determined by the reader. As such, there are often a range of personal interpretations of the meaning inherent within a message across the audience spectrum.

Certain subcultural groups, for instance, may use visual signs and cues that are adopted from the parent culture, but are used to signify alternative meanings to their primary denotative signification. Examples might include the appropriation of expensive high fashion styles by 'street' gangs and subcultures – think of hip hop, rap, punk or skinhead fashions, which draw on alternative uses for cultural signifiers, from sportswear, yachting or golf clothing to military outfits and workwear.

Similarly, major international brands can be used to signify something other than their original, intended use. Brands such as Nike, Starbucks, McDonalds, BP and Shell have seen their logos used variously by activist and political groups as quick, shorthand indicators of the negative effects of global trade, sweatshop production lines, environmental damage and corporate greed – oppositional interpretations totally at odds with their original brand values.

house

home

Exercises: Design Literacy

Objective

The aim of these three related study projects is to allow you to investigate the principles of form and their function(s) in visual communication.

Within each project an emphasis is placed on exploring core research methods. This is intended to help you to critically develop your approach to both practical and theoretical aspects of your work.

In the investigation of visual language you will have the opportunity to re-evaluate fundamental design principles and to consider their relationship to content and meaning.

The intention is to provide you with an opportunity to reassess your own approaches to practice in a process that might be described as de-learning and re-learning.

Part 1: Object

This brief asks you to explore the specific shape that you have chosen from three simple geometric forms (circle, square or triangle), by producing a series of small-scale projects that investigate the attributes of visual form including:

Space and form: *Line, plane, mass, void*
Time and meter: *Rhythm, order, motion, sequence*
Light and colour: *Hue, tint, tone, saturation, transparency, opacity*

You should try to build a series of related practical experiments that demonstrate you have understood key factors in visual grammar such as: *mass, unity, fragmentation, meter, regularity, irregularity, motion, activity, passivity, space, order, randomness, sequence, continuity, interruption.*

Essential Reading
Batchelor, D. (2000) *Chromophobia*. London: Reaktion Books.

Brewer, E. C. & Rockwood, C. (2009) *Brewer's Dictionary of Phrase & Fable*. 18th edition. Chambers Harrap Publishers: Edinburgh.

Dondis, D. A. (1973) *A Primer of Visual Literacy*. Cambridge, MA: MIT Press.

Evamy, M. (2003) *World without Words*. London: Laurence King Publishing.

Gage, J. (1995) *Colour and Culture: Practice and Meaning from Antiquity to Abstraction*. London: Thames and Hudson.

Gage, J. (2000) *Colour and Meaning: Art, Science and Symbolism*. London: Thames and Hudson.

Kepes, G. (1944) *Language of Vision*. Chicago: Paul Theobald.

Leborg, C. (2006) *Visual Grammar*, 1st English edition. New York: Princeton Architectural Press.

Lupton, E. (1991) *The ABC's of Bauhaus: The Bauhaus and Design Theory*. New York: Herb Lubalin Center of Design and Typography, Cooper Union.

Lupton, E. & Phillips, J. C. (2008) *Graphic Design: The New Basics*. New York: Princeton Architectural Press.

Müller-Brockmann, J. (1996) *Grid Systems in Graphic Design: A Visual Communication Manual for Graphic Designers*. Zurich: Verlag Niggli AG.

You should also explore the application of colour to your formal investigations, testing, for example, the effect of: *addition, subtraction, complement, contrast, tint, tone, hue, saturation.*

Try to use methods that are not restricted to predictable outcomes by exploiting unfamiliar or untested media, locations, processes, materials, textures, formats, and so on.

Your investigations at all stages should be developed and documented with a view to producing a body of work that is based in analysis and developed in a systematic and organized fashion.

An important aspect of this part of the project and the next stage is that you concentrate on how you document each visual experiment or test and how

these are presented. The focus on the process and methods you employ and how you will document them is a fundamental consideration of the project.

You must remember to focus on the nature and manner of your enquiry rather than the outcome. At this stage of the project, the journey is more significant than the destination. Whilst it is important as a designer to develop your approach to producing effective solutions or answers, this project is more concerned with the questions you ask and how you communicate them.

Roberts, L. & Thrift, J. (2002) *The Designer and The Grid*. Brighton: RotoVision.

Wilde, J. & R. (1991) *Visual Literacy: A Conceptual Approach to Solving Graphic Problems*. New York: Watson-Guptill.

Wong, W. (1993) *Principles of Form and Design*. New York: Wiley.

Further Reading
Crow, D. (2010) *Visible Signs: An Introduction to Semiotics in the Visual Arts*, 2nd edition. Worthing: AVA Publishing SA.

Heller, S. & Pomeroy, K. (1997) *Design Literacy: Understanding Graphic Design*. New York: Allworth Press.

Lupton, E. & Abbott Miller, J. (1996) *Design Writing Research: Writing on Graphic Design*. London: Phaidon.

Rudolph, A. (1954) *Art and Visual Perception: A Psychology of the Creative Eye*. Berkeley: University of California Press.

Exercises: Design Literacy

Part 2: Context

Brief 2 requires you to explore the cultural contexts surrounding the object you have been working with and to critically examine its uses in a representation, as a sign, symbol, icon or metaphor. You should develop a series of related briefs; investigating a range of contexts, meanings and values of the shape.

The questions you might ask are up to you, though they might include the following, for example:

· How have the meanings of the shape been constructed in social and cultural contexts – and why?

· What is the relevance of the shape to other fields, such as gestalt, mathematics or language for example?

· What is the relationship of the shape to historical, contemporary, linguistic, semiotic, philosophical, psychological, sociological, political, economic, technological or other frameworks?

In generating design concepts you should consider:

· How can you present a new and critical perspective to something very familiar and in the process challenge assumptions concerning it using design methodologies?

· How can you use it to generate insightful, novel, unpredictable, communicable ideas?

Working Process

You should begin both assignments by attempting to generate a number of ideas or *propositions* for your investigations. Try to put down on paper as many responses to the briefs as possible and as much of your existing knowledge as you can.

You should not look for final resolutions until the end stages of the project. Initially, you are asked to generate a series of visual responses and construct practical experiments that record your investigations. You are more likely to produce insightful, unpredictable and purposeful work by seeking alternative iterations, developing and redeveloping both ideas and forms while maintaining a critical perspective.

You will also examine the object's functions and meanings by researching how they are constructed in diverse cultural contexts. You should make use of resources such as libraries, museums and galleries and share what you discover with your colleagues. Do not rely on unsubstantiated Internet sources for your information.

Your practical experiments, contextual investigations or other researches should be diverse but should also develop progressively as a series of alternative critical responses to the object provided.

Each will benefit from a committed investment of time, energy, thought, craft, diligence, materials, attention to detail and production values.

You can use any appropriate media you wish, and should not hesitate to use methods that you are not familiar with.

Part 3: Output

Brief 3 should be undertaken when the two previous stages have been completed. This brief requires you to revisit and critically re-evaluate your earlier investigations with a view to focusing on a single, conceptual aspect of them.

You should develop this to a final completed stage – a single piece of work (or a series of pieces) intended to communicate to a specified audience. Emphasis should be placed on generating a range of ideas and investigating possible ways to effectively communicate them. The intention is not merely to amplify earlier work but to use Brief 1 and 2 as a starting point for generating a range of ideas that demonstrate you have now developed a critical conceptual understanding of the shape.

Your final third project might take the narrative form of a story, for example, and might be presented as an animation or as a traditional book employing words and images together.

You might however elect to explore the shape you have been working with in a more applied manner: investigating the shape in relation to visual identity and branding, for example.

It is important that you decide how you will work and in what context your work will be viewed. Remember, to be successful working in this way, it is important to establish the guidelines for how your project should be judged.

Learning Methods: Using Sketchbooks and Notebooks

Throughout the course you should initiate and progress your work by using a personal sketchbook, notebook and/or research folder that will allow you to work through your conceptual processes.

Use your sketchbooks to generate ideas, to record textual, contextual and visual researches (however messy) and to reflect upon each stage of the project. They are perfect locations to test visual research methods: visualization, proposition, analysis, interpretation and documentation.

3. Analysis and Proposition

Recording, evaluating and documenting a range of visual and verbal structures, languages and identities

Research and Design

Research methods can be defined as ways of approaching design problems or investigating contexts within which to work. This chapter focuses on thematic approaches to problem solving and the construction of rational and logical systems of design thinking. By improving their knowledge of existing visual conventions, together with the development and application of a personal visual vocabulary, designers are able to make more effective use of their perceptions and discoveries, and to work practically and creatively with reference to a wider cultural context. Systematic research methods encourage designers to develop a personal and critical point of view through the recording, documenting and evaluating of visual and verbal structures, languages and identities in the wider environment, and then applying those findings within their own work.

The adoption of a rigorous methodology that addresses the specific requirements of the brief and sets a series of boundaries within which to work on a broader investigation can help the designer to focus a project and define the exact problem, or series of problems, to address. Breaking the project down into a set of intentions, each with defined parameters and a predetermined level of background knowledge or experience on the part of the designer, makes the task more achievable and the goals of each stage of the process more explicit. Each of these areas will be explained in detail within this chapter, showing the developmental process of a strategic design methodology relevant to the context of the brief. Examples of work illustrating key concepts from both the professional and academic fields are included to guide you through each stage of the process.

Research

A critical investigation or a search or enquiry to discover new facts and information or to collect and collate old data in order to evaluate and test hypotheses or design proposals. This would encompass the study of a subject, employing the analysis of quantitative and/or qualitative data.

Research employs methods and schemes of testing to interpret events, facts or information, and is a process of observation, discovery and recording. In the context of graphic design, research provides the foundations of the design process of problem solving and visual communication. The research component of a graphic design brief can take a singular form in some projects, such as the collation of audience feedback to a proposal, or it can operate in a number of forms simultaneously, each body of research findings working together and in tandem to inform the overall approach to a project.

In recent years, graphic design has grown to accommodate a wide variety of approaches and intentions. Significantly, for a number of designers, research is a central and defining activity in their work. In these cases, research is more than an activity used to define effective visual solutions to a client's brief or design problem.

It instead becomes an outcome in its own right, informing a designer's or design group's approach, and generates a way of developing new ideas and techniques of thinking and making. The act of designing can in itself then lead to new discoveries and insights into the subject under investigation.

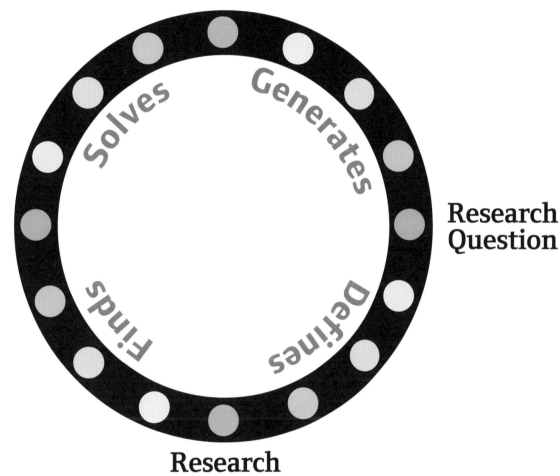

Problem/Idea

Generates

**Research
Question**

Defines

**Research
Methodology**

Finds

**Research
Outcome**

Solves

02 The Design Cycle >>
Design is an iterative process. While much design may be geared toward finding an optimum solution for a given problem, this process in itself raises further questions and contexts through which to develop alternative and innovative outcomes.

Pure Research
The investigation of graphic and visual languages in a propositional sense, rather than those which have a predetermined commercial application. Although this form of research may not lead to 'real world' practical solutions, this does not obviate the need for a thorough analysis of the context of the work in relation to potential audience and the stated project intentions.

The outcomes of pure research are propositional and offer potential visual solutions to as yet undefined questions – in some cases, they define the problem yet to be solved.

Applied Research
Applied research is the investigation of a practical problem, usually with the underlying intention of creating potential practical solutions.

Empirical Research
Investigation into a field of study that is based on direct observation of phenomena.

Deductive Research
Research which starts from the position of a general conclusion, and then searches for data to support it.

Research and Design

These examples will also help to define each specific area of investigation explored and undertaken by the individual designer concerned.

The first task for the designer is to identify what he or she is attempting to achieve with the project – a broad intention or set of intentions. Within commercial practice, this might be described in the brief as the message to be communicated, or the target market that a commercial enterprise wishes to engage with. In this instance, the work undertaken is a form of applied research. Alternatively, in an academic context the aim might be broader; such as the proposal of a concept, or an idea for the student to visually investigate and respond to. In this case, the work undertaken is a form of pure research. In either case, the terminology may vary (see diagram page 61), and the distinctions between different stages of the process may be more or less defined,

but the breaking down of the proposal into separate areas of investigation and the definition of a project rationale is a useful preliminary exercise. Any design brief can be broken down into three areas for specific interrogation: a field of study or context of the project, a project focus (often described as the research question) and a research methodology.

The field of study (where will the work be situated, what already exists in relation to the problem being investigated, and what function will the end result fulfil?) describes the context for the work. This could be the field of wayfinding and signage within information design, or an audience-specific magazine page layout. First, the designer must research their field of study, to acquire knowledge of what already exists in that area, and the range of visual languages that can be directly associated with the specific target audience or market for the design.

Practical Problems

A practical problem originates in the real world and is related to pragmatic issues, and conditions such as cost, production and technology. It may also be influenced by its context, for example, the need to explore legibility and typographic form in relation to public signage for the visually impaired. This is an applied area of research and investigation, in that the solution itself may lie in constructing or posing a specific

research problem. The outcomes of applied research are tangible and offer real world or commercial solutions to already existing needs.

Research Problems

A research problem is typically developed in response to a subject or theme that the designer does not know or fully understand. A research problem may arise from, or be motivated by, a practical problem to be resolved – a field of study.

This then helps to define the project focus of the research and provides a specific question to be explored.

The research, investigation and development – the body of knowledge and understanding gained through research – is then applied to a practical situation or problem. Sometimes this is referred to as pure research and its outcomes are frequently conceptual, for instance in the development of an

appropriate visual vocabulary for a specific theoretical context.

03 Design Process Stages >>
Design requires the adoption of appropriate methods as a response to a defined question or hypothesis. The gradual 'narrowing down' of the field of operation, and the refinement of a specific question, allows the designer to adopt an effective working rationale.

Research and Design

This would normally be done through a visual audit or survey of the proposed design context.

The designer needs to consider both the external position of their intended work (the explicit aim of the communication itself) and its internal position (the relationship between this particular piece of visual communication and others within the same context). This is very important, as contemporary cultures are saturated with advertising, information graphics, site-specific visual identities and images related to entertainment or decoration. If a piece of graphic communication is to be displayed within this arena, the designer needs to be aware of how it relates to competing messages, and how the problems of image saturation or information overload might be resolved in order to communicate effectively. Of course, the designer will become more familiar with a specific field of study through professional experience.

By building a relationship with a particular client and their audience, the designer can learn which forms of communication are likely to be more (or less) effective. Field of study research then becomes more intuitive, based on prior experience, accumulated knowledge and learning, and the designer can move more quickly toward an appropriate project focus and methodology.

Choosing a Research Model

Field of study research takes a variety of forms, dependent on the intention of the proposed work. Market research methods, such as intensive visual audits of existing material, might be appropriate to some briefs, whereby the designer seeks out other work in the same field and analyses and compares the visual forms of communication relevant and readable to a specific audience.

Types of Research
There are several approaches to research often undertaken in relation to a graphic design brief. Some simple definitions by Meredith Davis include:

Descriptive Research
Observes and describes phenomena.

Historical Research
Seeks to reveal meaning in the events of the past. Historical

researchers interpret the significance of time and place in ways that inform contemporary decision making or put current practices into perspective.

Analytical Research
Generates quantitative data that requires statistical assistance to extract meaning. Analytical research requires testing and estimation and is particularly concerned with relationships and correlations in an attempt to predict outcomes.

Experimental Research
Attempts to account for the influence of a factor in a given situation. Experimental research defines relationships of cause and effect by changing the factor to be studied in a controlled situation.

Meredith Davis
'What's so Important about Research?' Statements, American Center for Design (ACD), Vol.6, No.1 (Fall 1990)

04 Research Project Models >>
Design methodologies may involve the broad 'scoping' and definition of a problem prior to design action, or alternatively the evaluation and refinement of a question through physical interventions within the field of study.

Field of Study → **Focus** → **Methodology**

Context-Definition

Context: Field of Study

Focus: Research Question

Context-Experiment

Context: Field of Study

Focus: Research Question

Context-Definition

Initial work in this model usually involves a thorough analysis of a broad range of secondary research, mapping the territory to be investigated and determining the range of work that has already been done within the field. Once a solid understanding of the context has been reached, the focus and research question for the project can be determined, and a working methodology defined. Primary research is usually beneficial at this stage, in the form of direct surveys of target audiences and visual experimentation to test appropriate visual languages.

The results of these preliminary visual and contextual experiments can then help to define the specific project intention, together with an appropriate methodology that allows the testing of a range of potential outcomes.

Context-Experiment

Initial work in this model usually involves looser mapping of the territory to be investigated, an analysis of the range of work which has already been done within the same context, and a specified intention for the work within any revised context.

The focus for the project needs to be determined earlier than in the context-definition model, particularly through the definition of what the designer, and the client where appropriate, wishes to achieve. Distinct visual experiments to test appropriate visual languages and strategies are then conducted in order to determine a range of potential solutions. It is important that an overarching strategy is employed by which to critically evaluate and reflect upon the relationship between each individual experiment.

Research and Design

This could mean a review of comparative products or visual systems, working with a client to establish their position in the marketplace or their aspirations to communicate with a particular audience. In most cases, sophisticated visual languages already exist that attempt to engage those audiences, and the designer should become familiar with their vocabulary, even if his or her intention is to create a new form of communication that sets itself in opposition to that which already exists (i.e. what might be called an innovative or creative solution).

Cost implications are also important to consider at this stage of the project. The costs of materials, print reproduction or other media (web design, digital storage and so on.), labour and overheads all need to be taken into account against the intended budget for the project. The designer and client need to have a strong idea of the range of materials available – and, importantly, affordable – to them, and the implications of those decisions upon the design itself. If the budget can only cover the cost of two-colour printing, for instance, then those restrictions need to be put in place in advance and then turned to the designer's advantage in seeking innovative responses to the range of techniques and materials available.

The Project Focus

Once the field of study has been defined and broadly analysed, the next stage in the design process is to specify a project focus (what will the specific context and function of the work be within the wider field of study already defined?) and research question (a refinement or redefinition of the original intention, or a hypothesis or proposition to test).

Topography
A detailed description of spatial configuration. The word could be employed to describe a process of mapping, documenting or recording, often with particular reference to what is occurring below the surface. Useful in graphic design research to describe an underlying approach to a project or a working method or process.

Typology
The study and interpretation of types – for instance, a person, thing or event that serves as an illustration or is symbolic or characteristic of something. The phrase also relates to the organization of types and their classification for the purposes of analysis.

05 Process Terminology >>
There are many ways to describe the design process from inception to solution, dependent on the wider cultural or professional context of the work.

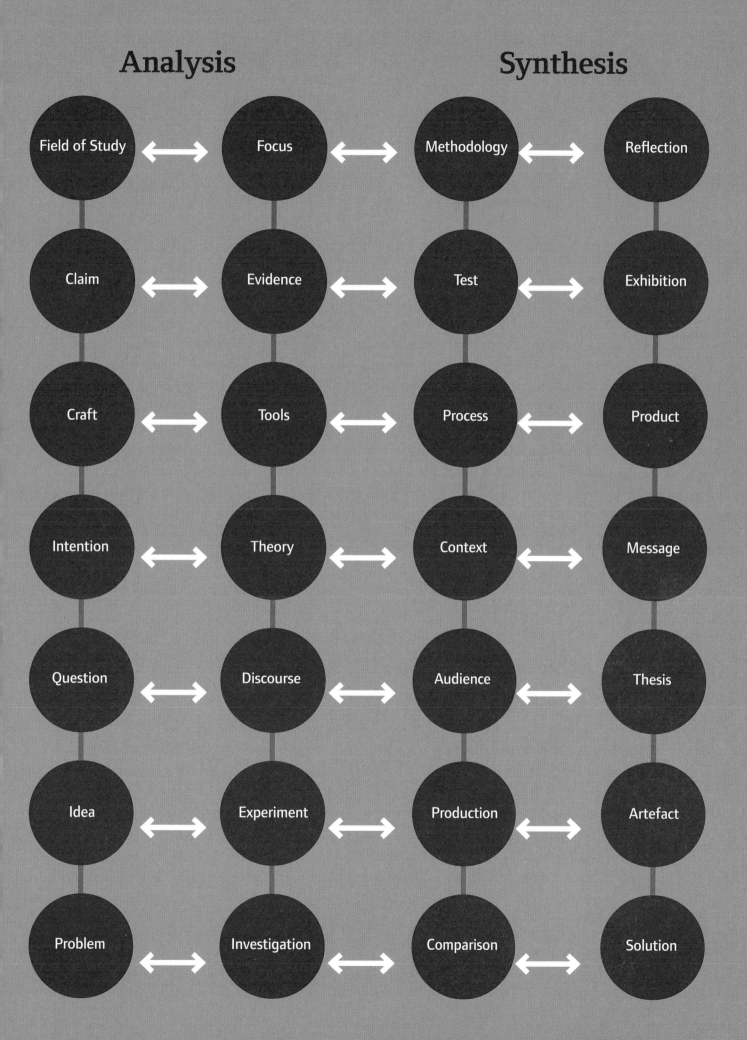

Research and Design

Once the designer has become familiar with the broader intentions of the brief, a specific project research question is needed to demarcate the exact intentions of the work to be undertaken. At this stage, the designer should be able to describe the message that is to be communicated to a specific audience, or within a specific context, and the aims and objectives of that communication. For instance, to persuade the receivers of the message to act in a particular way (e.g. buy this product, go to this event, turn left at the next junction), or to clearly communicate a particular emotion or identify with a subcultural group.

The focus and specific research question may change during the lifespan of a project, becoming broader and then being redefined in an ongoing process of critical reflection and reappraisal. There are a number of ways in which the narrowing down and refining of a project focus might take place. Two useful models for the designer to use in order to ascertain the context of their work and define a particular research question are set out diagrammatically on page 59.

The first research model, which we will term the 'context-definition' model, emphasizes the investigation of a field of study. In this model, the designer attempts to become more expert within the field of the brief and the project focus is defined in response to an identifiable need within that area. The second model, termed 'context-experiment', still requires the designer to undertake a broad preliminary analysis of the field of study, but the practical work on the brief itself begins earlier in the process. Usually this is done through a series of tests or experiments, which can be evaluated within the field of study, leading to a redefinition of the research question dependent on the results gathered. It is important here for the designer to not lose sight of the original project

Analysis
The stages of a graphic design project that involve the collection and collation of data and the analysis or interrogation of existing properties and conventions therein. There are many ways to describe this aspect of a design project, dependent on the specific area of the design profession within which the work is being undertaken. For instance, within an academic environment, where a project might be described as occupying the arena of pure research, the analytical stage of the project might be described as the broad investigation of a field of study and the further specification of a project focus.

In models of applied research, these terms could be supplanted with 'problem' and 'investigation' or 'idea' and 'experiment' – in each case, this stage of the project involves the gathering of background material and the establishment of the key themes and intentions of the brief.

Synthesis
Once a clear context and content of the design brief have been established, the designer is able to bring together secondary and contextual research findings with a range of experimental and practical methods of production in order to develop the final outcome or artefact. Again, these terms vary depending on the background of the project and the position of the designer, but 'synthesis' in each case implies the use of knowledge gained through research and the testing of alternative production methods in the planning and formation of creative and inventive design resolutions.

intentions, and to work through their experiments in a systematic way. The context experiment model will inevitably lead to a number of 'failed' experimental outcomes, as each small 'test' is an attempt to gain feedback in the definition of the project focus. In fact, if an experimental piece of visual communication is unsuccessful when tested with a target audience or in a specific context, then this should still be seen as a positive exercise in gathering information on the project focus and identifying directions with less potential for further development. By determining what does not work, as well as what potentially does, the designer is in a far better position to arrive at a more successful resolution.

A Plan of Action

Once the problem has been identified, the next step concerns the choice of appropriate research methods (how will the designer research and develop the project in response to the context and intention?). A research methodology is simply a set of self-imposed rules by which the designer will approach or engage with a project or brief. Once the intention of the work has been clearly stated, together with a detailed mapping of the field of study and the definition of a focus and research question, the designer needs to outline exactly how he or she intends to go about developing the project and testing ideas in order to create an effective solution to the brief – a plan of action.

The intention here is to develop systematic ways of working that lead progressively to a more successful outcome, based on experiments and visual testing, materials investigation and audience feedback, and the goal is to produce a piece of graphic design which is effective, useful or engaging.

Analytical
Adjective relating to analysis
(n.) – the division of a physical or abstract whole into its constituent parts in order to examine their interrelationships.
The New Collins Dictionary and Thesaurus – HarperCollins (1992)

As a design method, this involves the designer becoming more familiar with the specific message or intention of the brief, the audience, appropriate visual language and the requirements of the client.

Propositional
Adjective relating to proposition
(n.) – a proposal for consideration, plan, method or suggestion.
The New Collins Dictionary and Thesaurus – HarperCollins (1992)

This usually takes the form of a hypothesis or what might be termed a qualified assumption, supported by some form of material evidence. Within graphic design, this means the definition and testing of a range of alternative potential solutions.

Design involves both aspects of research. Designers need to be aware of the context within which their work will be read, and the possibilities offered by audience familiarity, materials and budget constraints. The solution also needs to be innovative – offering a new way of presenting the information.

Different graphic design projects may involve each of these areas of research to a greater or lesser extent. The range and application of appropriate research methods is dependent on the brief or research question, the specific qualities of the message to be communicated, project budget and timescale, and the relationship between client, designer and audience.

Claim

Qualific

06 Claim and Evidence >>
Central to any design research
activity is the relationship between
the viability of the research
question and the methodology
employed in the exploration of the
subject under examination.

It is useful to consider this notion
as if one was constructing an
argument. The rhetorical aspect of
graphic design is a central defining
feature of the discipline. To create a
successful argument, it is important
to be explicit in two key factors;
the **claim** that is being made by
the person putting forward the
argument, and the **evidence** that
he or she provides to support their
claim (the **qualification** of the
validity of the argument).

The assertion – the claim that the
designer is making – should be
both substantive and contestable.
The contention proposed should
be supported by relevant and valid
evidence. This evidence should be
introduced in stages; in some cases
it should be treated as if it were a
sub-claim and may itself need to be
supported by further evidence.

The qualification of the design
proposal – the evidence to support
the claim – helps to fulfil a number
of requirements in a successful
design. It can help substantiate
the choices made by the designer
when presenting the work to the
client, give greater credence to the
visual vocabulary adopted, and
lead to a more thoroughly tested
and therefore, probably, more
successful outcome.

→Evidence
ation

'Pure' information exists for the designer only in abstraction. As soon as he begins to give it concrete shape, to bring it within the range of experience, the process of rhetorical infiltration begins.

Gui Bonsiepe
Visual/Verbal Rhetoric – Ulm 14/15/16 (1965)

Feedback and Evaluation

The adoption of a series of strong and appropriate research methods should help the designer to make work that can be justified in terms of the processes used, and can be predicted to get closer to this goal. It is also important to plan the work in advance, including a rough schedule identifying when the designer expects to undertake each experiment, and the proposed deadline for finishing the project. Whether within the areas of commercial graphic design or design study, deadlines are usually given as a part of the brief. Even where this isn't the case, for instance when a designer is conducting a personal visual investigation, it is still important to plan a time frame for the project.

'Experimentation' has become something of a buzzword in contemporary graphic design. An experiment is a test or investigation, planned to provide evidence for or against a hypothesis – an assumption that is put forward in order to be verified or modified. When a designer is working towards producing a piece of work, a series of visual tests or design experiments might be useful in gathering feedback on new ideas and forms of communication.

However, experimentation is not a virtue in itself, it has to operate within a set of precise guidelines, delineating the intention and context of the experiment, together with the ways in which feedback will be gathered and results will be measured. In short, a design hypothesis might be that the creation of a particular visual form will communicate a particular message to a given audience. An experiment to test this hypothesis would then involve creating variations of that form and gathering feedback from target audiences or experts within that particular field of design in order to measure the relative success or failure of the work to communicate as intended.

Authorship
The involvement of the designer in the mediation of the message to an audience. It can be argued that through the creation and mediation of visual messages, the designer has an equal role to play in the ways in which a piece of visual communication is read as the originator of the message itself.

The designer, as a form-giver or channel through which the message is passed, can play a key role in actually shaping the content of the message. Some design theorists have borrowed the notion of the *auteur* from film theory in an attempt to build on this notion, while others have been provoked into a heated response that foregrounds the neutral role of the graphic designer within a commercial arena.

Theories and Hypotheses
A theory is a comprehensive and explanatory framework or system of concepts – it is a set of rules or procedures formulated in the mind. A theoretical model or plan can generate a number of hypotheses – these are assumptions or suggested explanations for a group of facts or phenomena that are used as a basis for further investigation and verification, or are accepted as likely to be true in the case of a *working hypothesis*. A hypothesis is a specific prediction or supposition, typically derived from a theory, which the researcher can use as a basis for testing, benchmarking or as a model to react against in the formulation of alternative strategies or practices.

Another key question to consider at this point is, how do we measure results or quantify our findings? In setting up a series of 'experiments', which might involve trial runs with alternative visual strategies in response to a defined problem, how is the designer to go about gathering feedback in order to evaluate which of the visual applications is the more successful? There are a number of ways to respond to these questions.

Market research, especially in relation to product advertising and marketing, has developed some successful methods of testing materials and form through the use of focus groups, statistical analysis of surveys and audience observation techniques. Some of these techniques can be linked to anthropology and the study of human interaction within social groups, whilst others derive from more scientific methods of data gathering and quantitative analysis.

It is also important to understand the differences between quantitative and qualitative methods. The designer will often use both forms of analysis, and their application may prove more or less useful depending on the brief and target audience, but the methods themselves are distinctly different.

Quantitative analysis is based upon mathematical principles, in particular statistical methods of surveying and interrogating data. By producing a number of visual forms to test, the designer can place these objects in specific locations in order to 'count' positive and negative responses from a target audience. This could mean conducting a survey using multiple choice questions devised to score against a set of criteria. The data gathered could then be converted into numbers and analysed statistically to find the most successful visual form.

The idea that a designer was an artiste first and a communicator second (or third) was quaint at the outset but has offered diminished returns over the long term. Although individual personality routinely plays a key role in visual communication, it must be the result, not the goal, of solving design problems.

Steven Heller
'The Me Too Generation' in *The Graphic Design Reader* (2002)

Feedback and Evaluation

Of course, as the size of survey group or sample increases, we anticipate that the results will become more accurate.

However, if the survey questions are not strictly controlled or specific enough, there can also be a tendency for results to become blurred. Human responses to questions are not the same as results gathered within scientific experiments – reactions to a visual message ('I quite like it', as against 'I like it a lot') cannot be weighed in the same way as, for instance, the mass of a residue formed by the reaction between two chemical elements. People often have a tendency to score their reactions within the middle range of the options available to them, which can result in a statistical steering of data away from any radical or innovative propositions and toward a natural median or average. This can lead to an overemphasis on that data that is largely contained within a

conservative, middle ground set of replies, perhaps erroneously indicating a resistance to change.

Counting the Cost

Quantitative methods do apply quite strongly, however, in the areas of materials investigation and technology (which is explored more fully in Chapter 6: Process and Materials). If a piece of work is to be produced in multiple numbers (as almost all graphic design is), then the criteria for choice of materials – its resistance to age deterioration or discolouration, distortion, stability and its fitness for purpose – can be subject to quantitative evaluation. Materials testing (through the use of alternative substrates and surfaces on which to print, or technologies to view online data) is an important area of design experimentation, and the results of research within this area can usually be measured with some degree of accuracy.

Conducting Surveys

Surveys can be a useful method for generating and gathering data in response to a proposition or research question – a hypothesis that the designer is seeking to evaluate, verify, prove or disprove.

However, a great deal of care needs to be taken by the author or designer with regard to the specific nature of questions asked within a survey, and the range of anticipated interpretations and analyses of feedback received. The way that a survey is introduced to prospective respondents, the framework for the questions, the language used (which could imply the kind of response desired by the questioner) and even the tools and means of mark-making offered can all have a major effect on the kinds of responses received.

Similarly, the cost implications involved in the selection of alternative materials and production methods can be compared and measured against the constraints of the project budget. When a piece of work is to be manufactured as a long production run, especially in printed form, the costs involved in even the smallest design decision are magnified accordingly – from the cost of ink and paper to the time and labour involved in folding, collating, cutting and finishing the final artefact. Printers set up their machines to operate using the most common formats and production runs. This usually implies a reliance on standard ISO (International Organization for Standardization) or imperial paper sizes and colour palettes (the CMYK four-colour process or Pantone spot colours, for instance).

If the designer chooses to work outside of these standards, set-up times for production will be longer and the costs will, therefore, increase. As such, the economic aspects and implications of the project need to be planned carefully in advance, and quantitative methods can be useful for the designer in calculating the budget for the project.

Qualitative analysis in design, on the other hand, is based on a range of subjective readings and responses by a viewer – though this may be the audience as receiver or the designer as originator of the message, depending on the stage at which the analysis is appropriate to the project – and is implicit in the surveys and focus groups mentioned earlier in this section (see page 66–67).

Qualitative Analysis

Qualitative analysis is based on subjective responses to visual forms and the reading of graphic material by a viewer. Often this is done by the designer him- or herself, in the form of critical self-reflection. The reading of images and visual signs through semiotic analysis is, however, a qualitative act in itself: although the responses can be evaluated statistically as a form of quantitative analysis, the initial data gathered is based on human reaction to the visual forms and experiments presented, and is thus by definition personal and subjective.

Quantitative Analysis

Quantitative analysis is based on mathematical principles, in particular statistical methods of surveying and interrogating data. By generating a batch production of visual forms to test, the designer can place these objects in specific locations in order to 'count' positive and negative responses from a target audience. This could mean conducting a survey within the target audience group, perhaps with multiple choice questions devised to score against a set of criteria. The data gathered can then be analysed statistically to find the most successful visual form.

Languages and Identities

A key qualitative method for designers involves the analysis, or deconstruction, of designed artefacts. What this means in practice is the reading of explicit and implicit messages within a visual form, to determine the range of meanings that might be communicated to a prospective audience through the principles of connotation and denotation (see pages 46–47). If the principles of visual communication are broken down into the twin themes of the encoding and decoding of meaning (synonymous with the acts of writing and reading), then the range of implied messages and interpretations can be largely determined in advance. Graphic design usually operates within very specific boundaries, where the intention of the brief is made clear by the client or designer at the outset.

Certain vocabularies drawn from communication theories can help the designer to describe the range of activities involved in the process of visual communication. These methods are useful for the graphic designer, as they can help to build constraints into the visual message in order to guide the viewer toward the desired reading, rather than a misinterpretation, of the message. By understanding how the message might be received and understood by a range of different readers, the designer can try to avoid unintentional ambiguities and misreadings. These themes will be explored in further detail in Chapter 4: Theory in Practice and in Chapter 5: Audience and Message.

The establishment of graphic design as a subject and a discipline that has grown from its roots as a commercial activity to the current situation, where it is studied at postgraduate level and is itself the subject of research and numerous books, has been a rapid one, and it is worth reminding ourselves of the

Critical Thinking
In concise terms, critical thinking is an attitude towards visual communication that is grounded in theory and its relationship to making. It is more than a philosophical position: informed or engaged practice is less about the ways in which theory can inform practice – it is graphic design engaged in the theory of practice, or *praxis*, with an equal priority given to both the theoretical and practical concerns of the brief. As the American designer and writer Andrew Blauvelt has observed, *'graphic design does not begin nor end in the objects it makes.'*

Critical thinking could be described as an important aspect of reflective practice – the consideration of the effects and consequences of graphic design activities. In general, reflective practice in graphic design could be described as locating the practice of graphic design as the subject of graphic design. Reflection in a designer's approach could encompass critical thinking about the meaning, function and value of what is produced and its relationship to the intentions of the individual designer and their audience.

newness of the area. Depending on your definition of the discipline, it is only around one hundred years old and a good proportion of contemporary debate is largely still concerned with definitions, responsibilities and purpose. This is especially significant when compared to the relatively longer history of related and tangential areas to graphic design from which ideas and descriptive languages are borrowed.

Looking into Design

These 'loan ideas' from areas such as language and communication, for example, bring with them a form of words that allow the discussion of what Jorge Frascara has described as '…*visual communication design*' in a manner that transcends the limited trade or technical language of the past.

The newness of the subject and the ongoing adoption of ideas and language from outside the

graphic design discipline, have encouraged the idea that '…*design does not have a subject matter of its own – it exists in practice only in relation to the requirements of given projects*' as the designer, educator and writer Gunnar Swanson has written. Swanson also suggests that design is 'integrative' and that the lack of specific subject matter belies its real potential to bridge and connect many disciplines. This is at the heart of this project: *Visual Research* explores how methods and approaches to the practice of graphic design can be explored and explained.

Critical Reflection
The process by which the designer reviews a project outcome or evaluates the success – or failure – of an experiment, by testing its effectiveness against a predetermined set of criteria. These criteria may be either self-imposed or may be a part of the brief itself.

Within the commercial arena, market testing and measuring the effectiveness of a graphic message are often rigorously applied. Where the designer is working in a more speculative environment, for instance within a project centred on pure research, the means by which effectiveness can be determined must be measured against the project's stated intentions.

For instance, a project which sets out to make visible certain underlying characteristics of a text within a book would need to be evaluated in ways that reflect that specific objective. Readers could be asked to interpret the design in order to ascertain whether the implied meanings are made clear. The designer could also draw on contextual research that analyses the range of graphic languages operating within the same arena, thus describing the range of already accepted codes on which to build.

Key Concepts: Rhetoric

The concept of **rhetoric** is usually applied to literature and philosophy, and refers to the strategic use of language as a foundation for reasoned argument. The classical art of rhetoric involves a number of distinct phases which, in relation to visual communication design, may be described as: the discovery of ideas, the arrangement of ideas, the stylistic treatment of ideas and the manner in which the subject matter is presented. These correspond directly to graphic design methodologies such as concept, composition, style and format.

Rhetoric traditionally comprises a range of figures of speech, including irony, antithesis, metonymy, synecdoche, pun, metaphor, personification and hyperbole. It can be useful to compare some of these strategies with a range of similar methodologies used in visual communication, in order to differentiate approaches and to suggest alternative methods to explore. Rhetorical terms utilized in graphic design might include:

Irony – a sign is employed to convey an oppositional meaning or to communicate a contradiction. Humour may often be used to imply an ironic, satirical or contradictory position, with visual elements employed to highlight an underlying tension or incongruity often already familiar to the viewer.

Antithesis – contrasting terms are placed together in order to emphasize their differences. Graphic designers might use contrasting images or messages in order to produce a dramatic effect.

Metonymy – a word or phrase is substituted for another with which it is closely associated. An image or name could be replaced by a symbol that encompasses similar connotations, such as a crown representing a monarchy.

Pun – a play on words, quip or witticism that exploits ambiguities in meaning for humorous effect. A designer may deliberately choose to employ an image or symbol encompassing more than one direct meaning or denotation as a simple, light-hearted visual pun.

Metaphor – a word or phrase is applied to an object or action that it does not denote, in order to imply a certain characteristic. Designers may deliberately use the range of connotations of a sign or symbol to reinforce a particular value.

Personification – attributing human features and characteristics to animals or inanimate objects.

Hyperbole – exaggeration for the purpose of emphasis or dramatic effect. This may apply to the relative scale of type and image, for instance.

Case Study 02: **Emotionally Vague**

Some types of self-authored design work can be constructed in such a way that the design of the visual artefact is in itself a process of discovery. This project, by designer Orlagh O'Brien, sets out to gather feedback from a large range of respondents to a questionnaire asking how and where they experience emotions, representing patterns of commonly reported visceral experience, but firmly maintaining each person's idiosyncratic responses.

As a design project the work sits firmly in the realm of pure research, with the design outcomes generated directly from the feedback gathered from participants in the survey arranged and collated so as to reveal consistencies and shared or common responses. However, subsequent to publication of the project, market researchers and scientists specializing in affective research have expressed interest in developing this methodology further.

Though the data gathered could be seen as entirely subjective, by its very nature, and the visualization techniques as implying the application of qualitative methods, the range and sheer number of responses – there were 250 participants and a choice from 170 colours on the research palette – led to outcomes that can be read to an extent quantitatively as well as qualitatively. By employing a range of graphic design methods drawn from information design and typologies, together with creatively overlaying images to reveal patterns and commonalities, O'Brien was able to show how her respondents visualized their feelings through colour, point and line in relation to their own bodies.

Over time, careful refinement of the range and type of questions that were posed in the surveys allowed for more detailed and explicit responses from the participants.

Revealing Tropes

In simple terms the word 'trope' refers to an object, image or event that serves as a generic illustration of a common trend, which may be widely characteristic of a cultural group or society. Examples of tropes might include frequently occurring visual representations of common principles or messages within a group, dress codes, or styles and trends linked to a specific period or location.

This method of working as part of a research project could also be described as analytical research – in that it examines a large body of qualitative data and allows a comparative analysis to be made between a large number of individual responses to the survey.

O'Brien used the visual language of information design to make a series of speculative outcomes that collectively reveal idiosyncrasies

and commonalities in approach by participants in the survey, in some cases layering the data in order to reveal patterns in the visual responses gathered from the initial surveys (opposite).

The designer also highlighted the relationship between this working method and elements of branding: *'There was a conscious decision to create methods to gather point, line, colour and typography, as per*

the elements of a brand. You could say that it is a "reverse engineered brand" as the start point is the feeling, and the end point is the visual.' (Orlagh O'Brien, 2011).

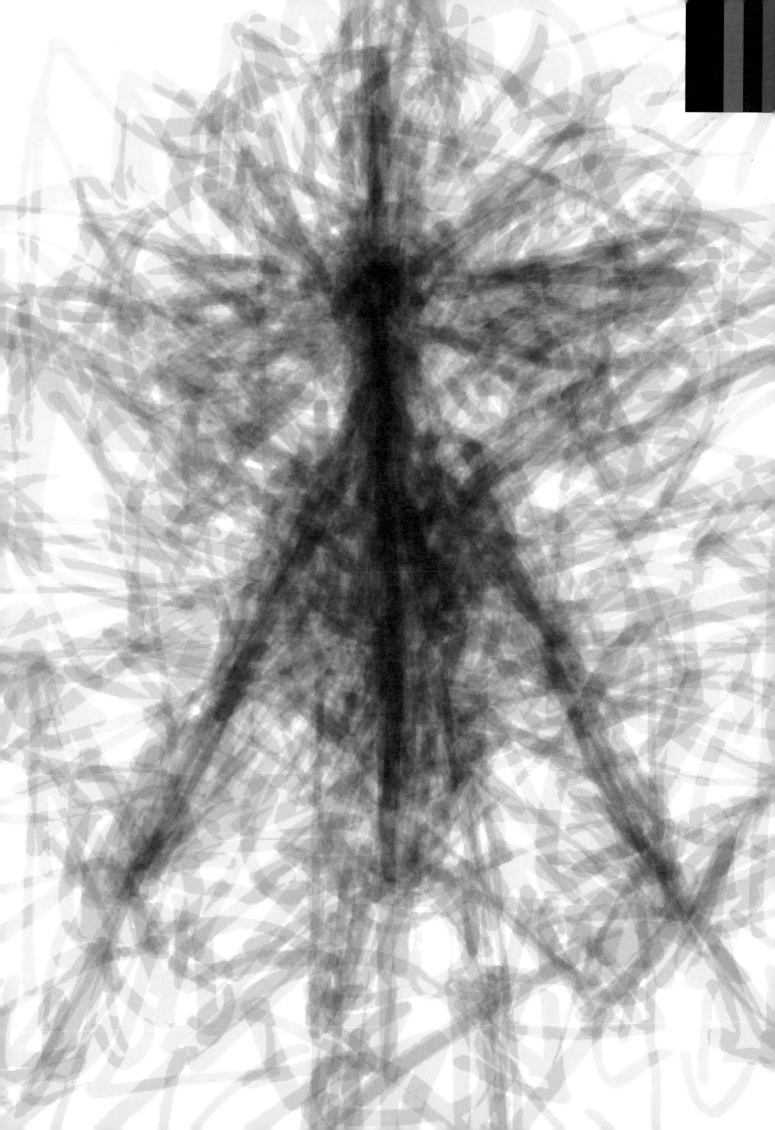

Case Study 02: Emotionally Vague

Although some control methods were set, such as the range of colours, the thickness of line-making tools and the diagrammatic framework within which marks were to be made, the designer was careful not to direct respondents toward preset or existing conclusions.

Refining the Research Techniques

O'Brien's initial research involved the development of a range of questionnaires, which asked participants to record visually where and how they felt particular emotions. Small 'test' surveys were then conducted to help the designer to evaluate results, refine the nature and phrasing of the questions and adjust the means by which participants could make their marks.

Initially, the survey also asked respondents to choose a pen from a limited range made available and to draw their own body, marking directly onto the image where, and how, they experienced particular emotions. O'Brien began developing methods to collate the information received, and to overlay visual responses in order to reveal consistencies and patterns across the range of individual answers. However, interpretation of the responses by categorization or themes was problematic. The designer as researcher felt that she was imposing her own subjective analysis on the drawings. A better approach was to avoid this completely by changing the methodology, aggregating, rather than categorizing the information gathered.

As the process of data collection also recorded personal information on the participants, the visual information could also be sorted and arranged by age, gender and nationality. Visual data was then collected identifying the location on participants' bodies where they felt those emotions, and the colour and direction that they associated with each feeling, in order to create a working database of visual material.

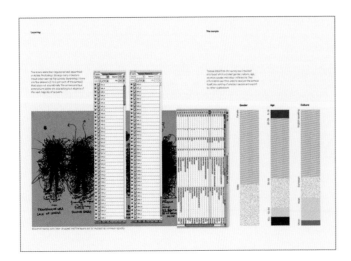

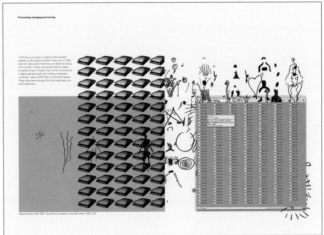

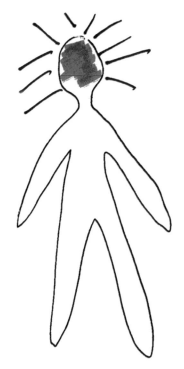

ANGER

JOY

LOVE

SADNESS.

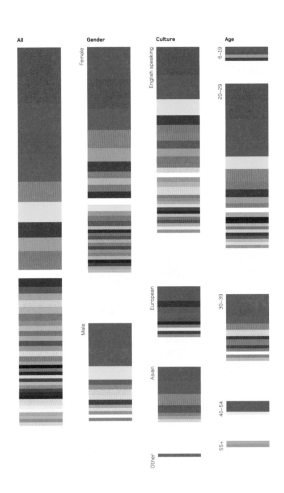

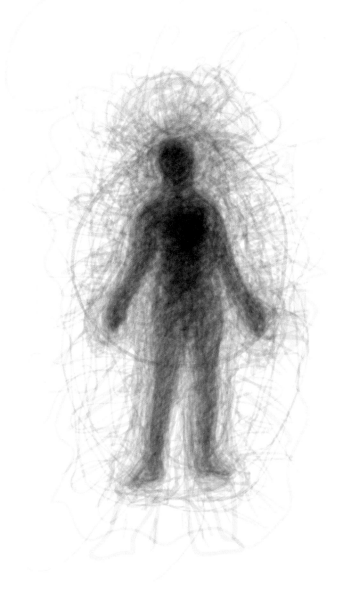

Refining the Data Set

As the survey was refined, it was redesigned to include a series of standard simple outline drawings of a human form, with headings such as joy, fear, sadness and love. Once collated, the body outline could be removed if necessary, to reveal the patterns of 'emotion marks' by themselves.

Marks revealing the location of emotions and the area that each feeling might occupy were surprisingly consistent across several hundred respondents (for example, see figure charting responses to 'love' above right). A further question to show the direction of the emotions produced dramatic visual outcomes, which were overlaid by the designer to create aggregate visual maps of the collective results. Respondents to the questionnaire were asked to choose specific colours that they associated with particular emotions from a colour chart, as well as describing where and how they felt those senses in relation to their own body. The results of these selections were then arranged by O'Brien in simple colour bars to reveal similarities and differences (see 'love' above left).

Questions about the visceral emotion ranged from very open (qualitative or subjective judgements), to particular (such as asking respondents to indicate point and direction in relation to the drawn figures on the page):
◊ : How do you feel these emotions in your body?
◊ : Where do you feel the emotions most?
◊ : Do your emotions have direction? # Yes ☑ No ☒
If yes please use the red marker to draw arrows describing each emotion.

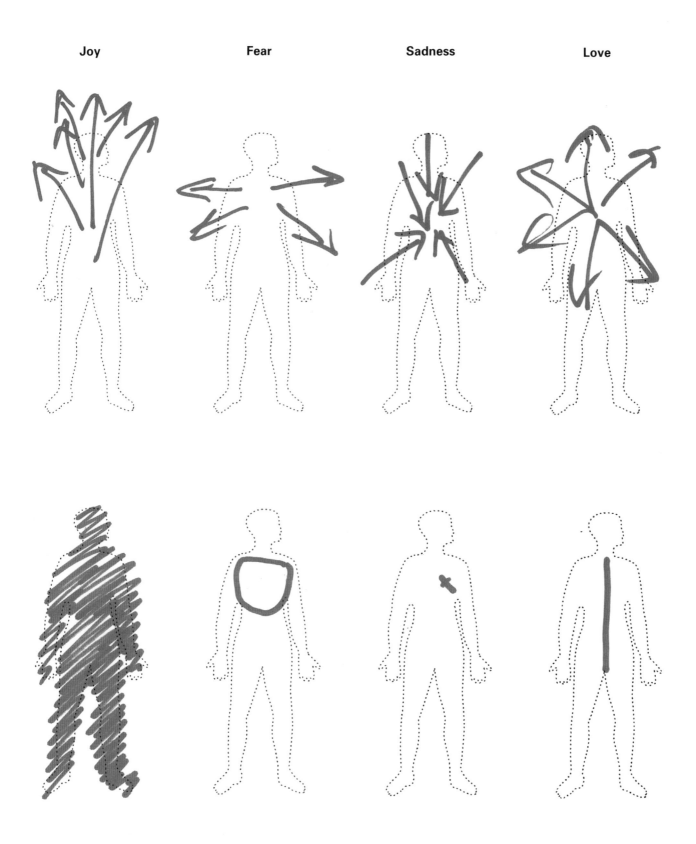

Joy   Fear   Sadness   Love

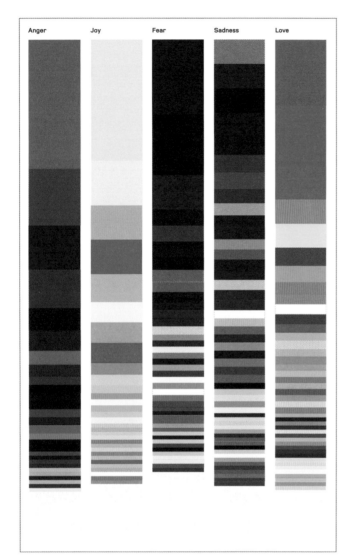

| Anger | Joy | Fear | Sadness | Love |

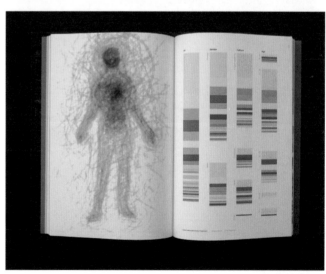

A Research Summary
The format of a book was chosen by O'Brien for the final project outcome (above and right). The original intention was to create five separate books, each showcasing the different language of a single emotion: joy, sadness, anger, fear and love. However, for the sake of greater cross referencing, a single book was chosen in the end. The final document is a summary of work produced within a set time frame for the project, and marks the findings reached at that point. The designer chose to view this as a 'staging post' within a longer investigation into the subject.

This visual material can be seen as a summary of the research process, with further testing and exploration detailed on the project website located at:
www.emotionallyvague.com

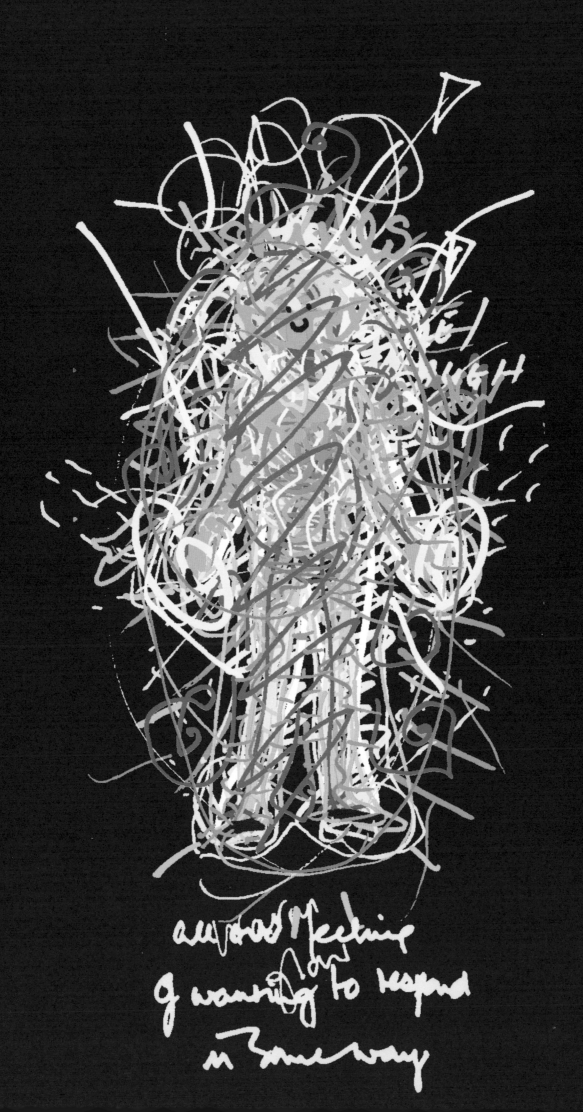

always flickering
& wanting to respond
in some way

Case Study 03: **Bibliospot**

An important aspect of design authorship and the self-initiated editing and visual communication of content lies within the field of information design. The designer can collect information and treat it in such a way as to emphasize new meanings that may be inherent in familiar content, or may find ways in which to reveal patterns, consistencies and the underlying organization within.

Designers have a responsibility to create work that is both accessible and understandable to its intended audience. As such, it is essential that research is conducted into the range of data to be visualized, the ways in which that data might reveal specific information, the target audience for a particular message and the contexts within which the work might be viewed and interpreted. Designer Alexandra Hayes chose to investigate a range of information design approaches to mapping a library system.

She was interested in developing a visual system that would help to identify and explain the content and context of archive material in a way that would make it more accessible. To achieve this, Hayes worked closely with St Bride Library in London, an archive of type and printing material that holds a complex and varied range of material within its extensive catalogue. She set out to create a system that could be transferable, allowing the user to compare different archives and libraries in terms of the quantities of bodies of information within different subcategories in their archives. Hayes' final outcome included a print- and web-based system for comparing and contrasting the relative size of bodies of archive material between different libraries.

Bibliospot Interactive
The total archive is visualized as one large circle, with ten distinct subcategories of classification. Each of these subcategories is then further broken down into another ten subsets, each of which again can be reduced to yet another ten smaller groupings in a decimalized system of organization (opposite).

By visualizing two archives side by side, the user is able to search the relative size and scale of holdings related to a specific subcategory within each library. The benefit of using an interactive format is that not all of the information needs to be viewable all of the time – this means additional variables can be introduced without creating a visual language that is over-complicated or confusing. The main function of the interactive tool is to enable users to discover which libraries hold the most items on a given subject by comparing their library spot size for each subject. It is aimed at researchers and academics and focuses on academic and specialist libraries.

The online system allows searching by subject using the hierarchical structure of a library classification system. This prototype uses the Dewey Decimal Classification (DDC) system, but it could easily be adapted to function in exactly the same way with any other hierarchical system – such as the Universal Decimal Classification (UDC) system. As the user clicks on a specific category spot, the screen-based system animates and orientates around that particular selection, thus allowing a means of scrolling through the various levels within an archive.

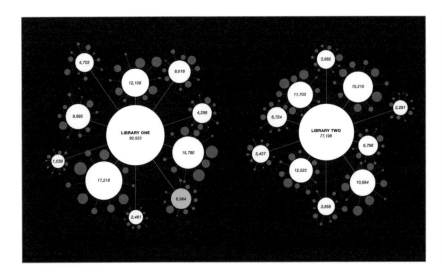

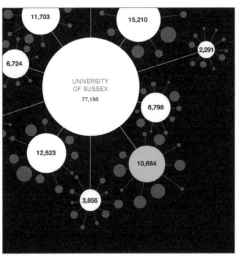

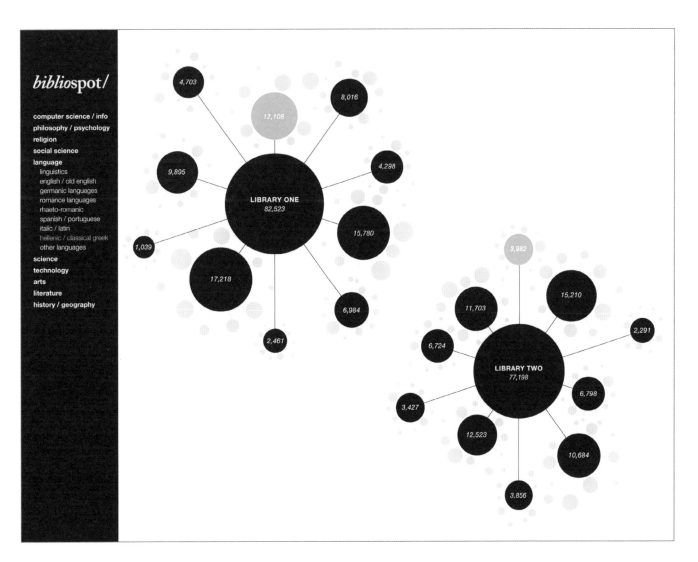

*biblio*spot/

computer science / info
philosophy / psychology
religion
social science
language
  linguistics
  english / old english
  germanic languages
  romance languages
  rhaeto-romanic
  spanish / portuguese
  italic / latin
  hellenic / classical greek
  other languages
science
technology
arts
literature
history / geography

Case Study 03: Bibliospot

Systems of Organization

Libraries and public archives organize their collections in a variety of ways including alphabetically by author, title, or by subject. In order to construct a system that would visualize library contents by subject, the designer needed to understand how each of these types of system operates. In order to make searching by subject as simple as possible, libraries use a classification system of coding and organizing that groups items with shared subjects to form classes and then allocates each class a specific number. Different types of system can include an alphabetical list of subjects, or subjects ordered within an internal hierarchy from more general to specific.

One of the most popular systems of library classification is the Dewey Decimal Classification (DDC) system, which organizes items into ten main classes, which are then subdivided into ten divisions and then each division into ten sections. This results in ten main classes, 100 divisions and 1000 sections. This system is hierarchical, meaning that the top ten classes are general subject areas, the 100 divisions slightly more specific and the 1000 sections are the most specific. Many libraries that use the DDC system to organize items by subject, also use it as a way of organizing the physical material in the library and therefore as a tool for locating items. Hayes' research suggested that it would be useful to incorporate a way of displaying the hierarchical nature of library organization by subject into the new visual system.

A Mathematical Problem

The St Bride Library classification system is structured around ten main classes, 100 divisions and 1,000 sections. However, unlike the Dewey Decimal Classification system used in many other libraries, it uses special classes with their own system of hierarchy. The library's online catalogue was used to collect data from the ten main classes and 100 divisions. By typing in each classification number it was possible for the designer to extract the number of entries held for each class. This gave a basic set of raw data. However, since 1980 the classification system has been in a constant state of revision and there are particular classes that are not represented accurately in the library catalogue. To make the data more realistic in terms of the library contents, Hayes worked closely with expert librarians at the library to revise the quantitative data in order to better reflect the 'reality' of the full archive. Once a suitable numerical database had been established, Hayes developed a range of potential iterations of a visual map of the archive (opposite).

The relative scale of each class or division was visualized by the area of each circle in the system. However, as some divisions had very small numbers of objects within them, and others very large data sets, a number of different mathematical and geometric approaches were explored. In fact, the largest class within the study contains 8,460 items whilst the smallest has just six. For the system to be successful, a factoring equation was necessary that would allow the smaller class to be visible while at the same time not leading to a huge visual domination by the largest class.

ABOUT
HOW IT WORKS
LIBRARY SEARCH
CLASSES

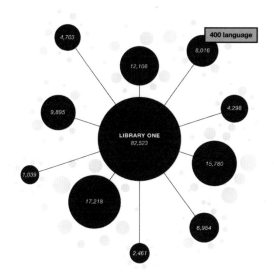

400 language

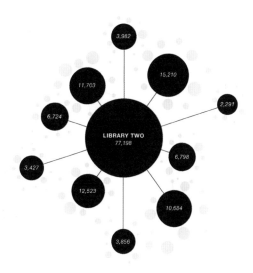

bibliospot/

| COMPUTER SCIENCE / INFO | RELIGION | LANGUAGE | TECHNOLOGY | LITERATURE |
| PHILOSOPHY / PSYCHOLOGY | SOCIAL SCIENCE | SCIENCE | ARTS | HISTORY / GEOGRAPHY |

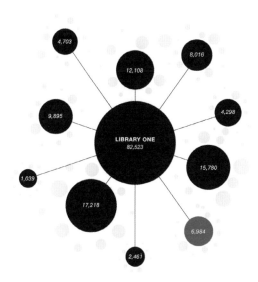

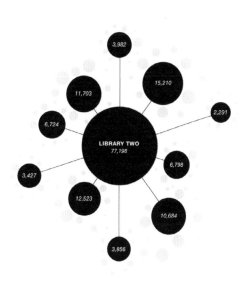

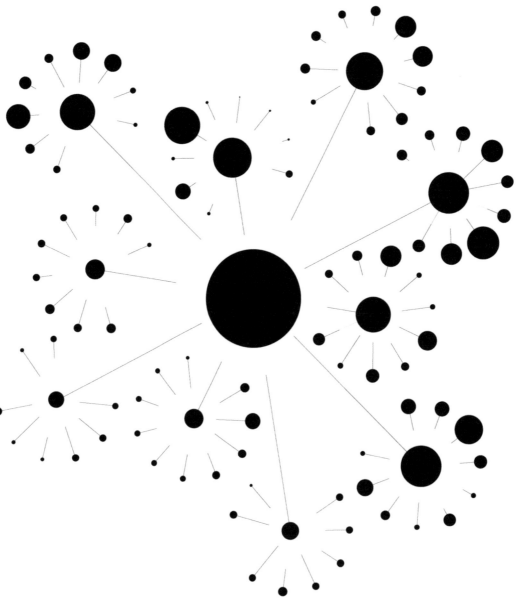

....

Initial Visual Tests
Early visual tests incorporated simple line and bar graphs, together with word clouds and typographic hierarchies displaying relative quantities of information within the archive (above and right), with the designer eventually choosing to develop a system based on connected circles (opposite). Text was also included within the smaller interlinking lines between levels of the system, determining each class, and with numerical indications relating to the quantitative value of the assigned catalogue number for each division (far right).

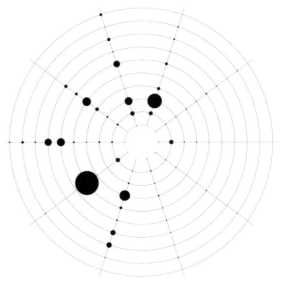

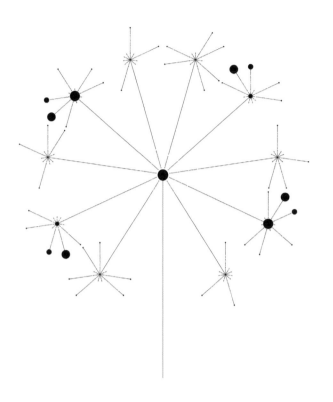

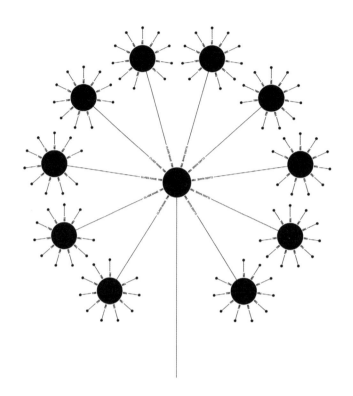

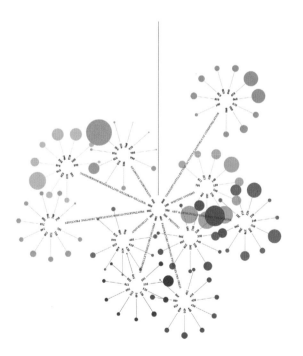

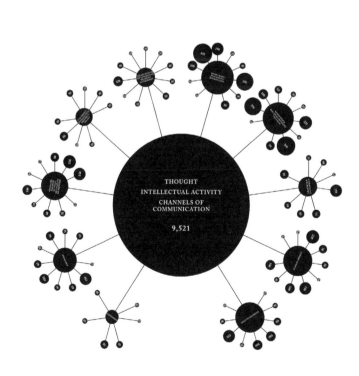

THOUGHT
INTELLECTUAL ACTIVITY
CHANNELS OF
COMMUNICATION

9,521

Growing Systems

Some of the more successful visual tests led to what could be interpreted as a more 'organic' structure. Whilst using the radial tree structure to show the classification hierarchy, Hayes eventually decided to position the ten main classes at varying distances from the central node, rather than statically arranged in an even circular orbit equidistant from the centre (above and right).

Other levels of relevant information could be used to base these relative distances on similar mathematical principles – for instance, the level of 'use' of each area over a period of time, or its position within the geography of the building. However, rather than relying on additional data or a system for this, the designer eventually chose to position them arbitrarily to give a more organic feel to the visualization and to imply possible

growth and change: an aesthetic decision to balance the more rigid and exact computational methods used in the rest of the system.

Colour systems were also explored in order to add further levels of specific information (opposite top left), but again were discounted as the range and number of variables was becoming too great to be readable without an extended key code to accompany the 'map'.

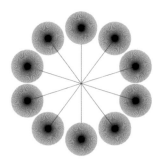

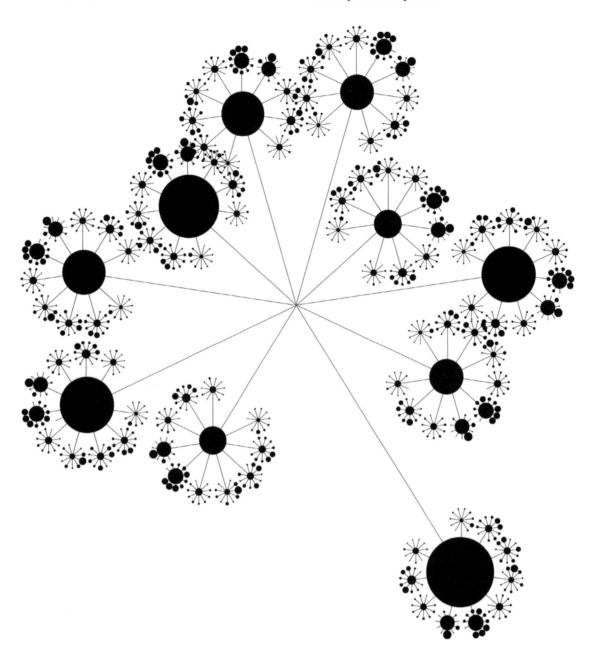

Revealing Structure

Mapping the collection using organic structures worked well both visually and on a conceptual level. The most successful visual test used a circle to represent each class (its size proportional in area to the value being represented) and then mapped the circles onto a radial tree structure (above). This enabled the viewer to easily see the structure of the classification system and also to compare the class values at each level within the structure. Relative links, interrelationships and quantitative information could be interpreted clearly and quickly using this simple visual system.

Having found a visualization technique that was working well, Hayes considered the possibility of increasing the level of complexity by adding more data. Having originally just collected data values from the top two levels of the classification system – the tens and the 100s, it became clear that there was a large amount of additional data that could be collected from the bottom level – the 1,000s. It seemed that by doing this, the level of information that could be extracted from the visualization would be significantly increased, and therefore it might be a more useful, and potentially more visually engaging, system.

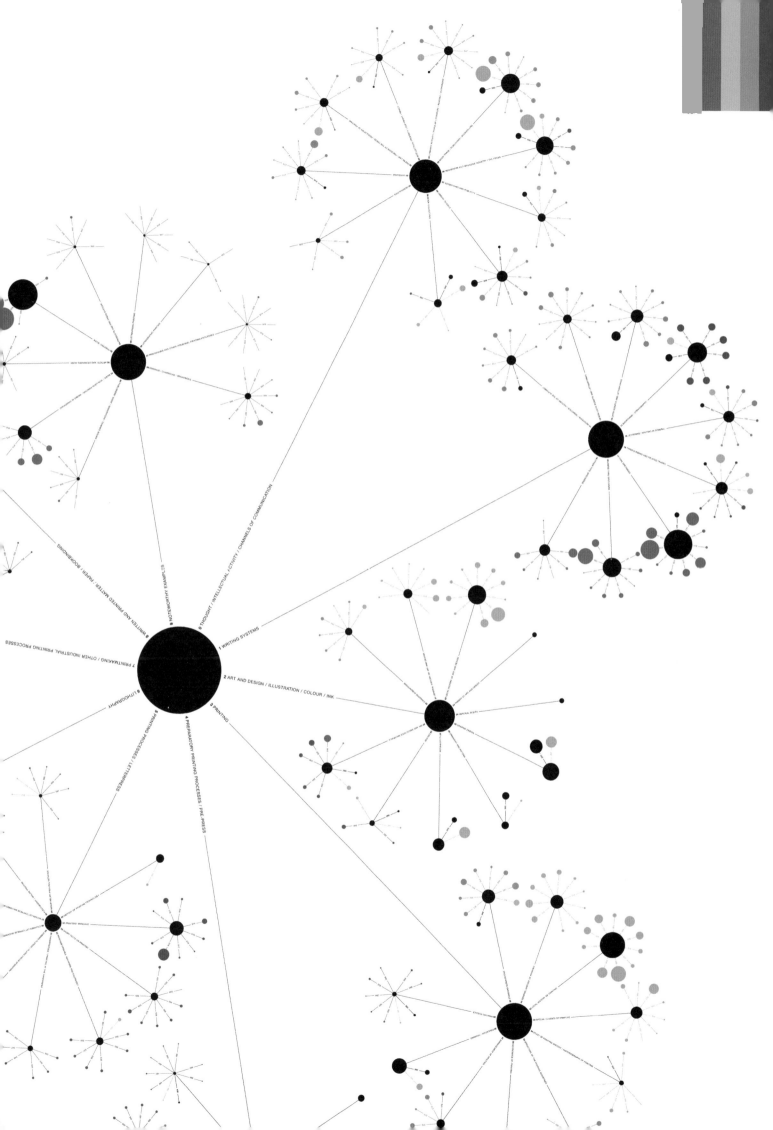

Key Concepts: Structuralism and Semiotics

According to the Swiss linguist Ferdinand de Saussure, language can be understood as a system of signs. In a series of lectures (the *Course in General Linguistics*), delivered at the beginning of the last century and published posthumously in 1915, Saussure proposed that the basic unit of any language is a **sign** or phoneme. A sign is made up of a **signifier** (an object) and a **signified** (its meaning).

For example, the word **bicycle** functions in the English language by creating the concept, or signified, of a mode of transport – a machine with two wheels that is powered by its rider and which is used for travelling from A to B. The relationship between the signifier and the signified is arbitrary. There is no logical or natural connection between the spoken sound or graphic representation and the concept of bicycle (this is known as duality). The connection or relationship is established solely in its use by English speakers – in the same manner that different sounding words describe the same object in different languages: *bicyclette* (French), *bicicletta* (Italian), *Fahrrad* (German), *polkupyörä* (Finnish), *rijwiel* (Dutch), *sykkel* (Norwegian), *reiðhjól* (Icelandic) etc.

Saussure was ultimately concerned with the structure *(langue)* rather than the use of language *(parole)*. This analytical way of thinking about the structure of language and meaning became known as **structuralism**. The basic unit of this structure, the sign, only has meaning because of its difference from other signs in the same system – the *langue*.

The study of signs is also known as **semiotics** – a term coined by the American philosopher, lexicographer and polymath Charles S. Peirce. His theories relating to language, logic and semiotics were developed during the same period as Saussure's. Peirce was concerned with the world we inhabit and how we use language and signs to understand this world. Peirce states that there are three principal kinds of signs: **iconic** signs, **indexical** signs and **symbolic** signs (see page 102). Iconic signs are likenesses that convey the idea of the thing they represent by imitating them, such as a photograph or drawing of something. Indexical signs convey information by 'indicating' their physical connection with the thing they represent, such as smoke to fire. Symbolic signs are general signs that have become associated with their meanings by conventional usage, such as the colours used in traffic lights.

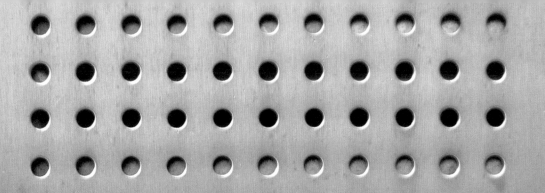

Fire

Police

FOR LIFT OR

FOR LIFT OR

TO REPORT AN EMERGENCY
1. LIFT COVER
2. PUSH BUTTON
3. ANSWER OPERATOR
YOU <u>MUST</u> ANSWER TO GET HELP

FDNY

Exercises: Design Analysis

Objective

The aim of this project is to develop your methods and visual thinking as tools of analysis. The outcome of this exercise is not necessarily an answer, instead it demonstrates that a good research question enables a better understanding of what is being investigated.

A typology is simply the study of types: a classification of similar things that have common characteristics or traits (see page 60). In the context of graphic design and research this can be understood as the creation of a system that allows a process of comparison to reveal patterns and connections that may not have been obvious to the viewer when they first encountered the body of material being analysed or organized.

This project will require you to explore the use of the typological classification of objects in constructing meaning. It is designed to highlight the role of collecting, archiving and taxonomy as fundamental features of research and analysis.

The project will provide the opportunity to gather data in a specific subject area chosen by you. It will allow you to develop useful skills in documentation, comparative analysis and inventive categorization and classification.

Designing a typology will introduce you to a useful method for research that can be applied to other projects, either as a working method in itself or as a process through which to discover a critical position and research question in relation to the material under investigation.

Key Texts

Bailey, K. D. (1994) *Typologies and Taxonomies*. Thousand Oaks, CA: Sage Publications.

Dion, M. (1999) *Tate Thames Dig*. London: Tate Gallery.

Harvey, C. (1995) *Databases in Historical Research: Theory, Methods and Applications*. London: Palgrave Macmillan.

Klanten, R. (2008) *Data Flow: Visualising Information in Graphic Design*. Berlin: Die Gestalten Verlag.

Klanten, R. (2010) *Data Flow v.2: Visualising Information in Graphic Design*. Berlin: Die Gestalten Verlag.

Perec, G. (2008) *Species of Spaces and Other Pieces*. London: Penguin Classics.

Streijffert, C. (1998) *Carouschka's Tickets*. Stockholm: Testadora.

Tufte, E. (1997) *Visual and Statistical Thinking: Displays of Evidence for Decision Making*. New York: Graphics Press.

Part 1: Gather Materials

You need to gather the materials for your collection. This will comprise a minimum of 15 pieces, which can take any form. It may involve collecting physical objects or it could be a documentation of a particular set of information using, for example, photography. Think laterally and creatively about what sort of content can be 'collected' and arranged in specific sequences.

Part 2: Describe and Explore

You will need to describe why you chose your particular subject area, as well as your initial observations and thoughts about the collection.

You should then begin exploring the ordering of your body of material. Working at A3 size, using a photocopier or laser printer only, you must produce at least five variations, demonstrating at each stage a different approach to organizing your collection. Take into account values such as scale, material, place of origin, function and so on.

Part 3: Presentation

Begin to explore how best to present the organized material in visual form. This may not necessarily take the form of a series of photographic images but might be more abstract in its presentation: replacing numbers or values with colours or shapes, for example.

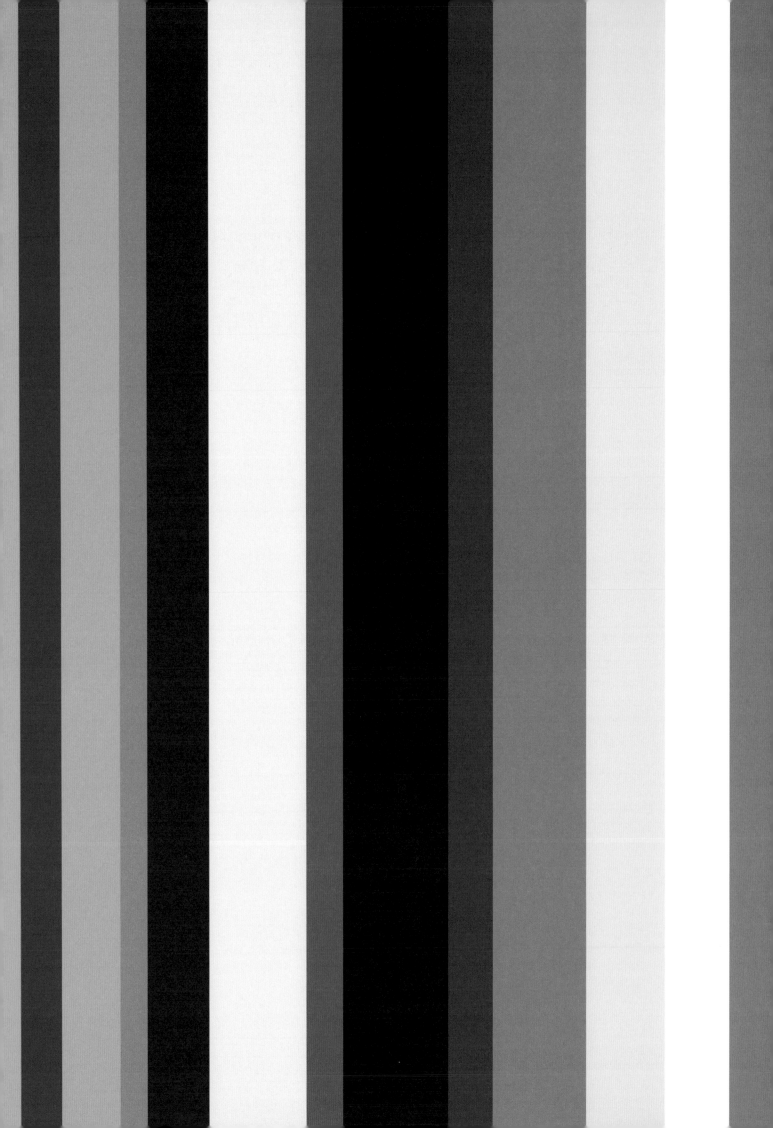

4. Theory in Practice

The deconstruction of visual work and the development of new design strategies and methods

Engaging with Visual Research

Visual research covers two main themes when related to what might be termed analytical and propositional methods – the deconstruction and interpretation of existing visual works and the development of new design strategies and methods. In order to develop tools for the analysis of design objects and artefacts, it is necessary for the designer to become familiar with terminology borrowed from a range of disciplines outside of the traditional role of the graphic designer. Some of these terms might be introduced to the design student as part of their wider cultural studies or visual culture and theory programme, but are often kept distinct from the range of practical activities within the design studio itself.

However, it is important for the designer to understand the vocabulary associated with the analysis of texts – by which we mean both visual and textual forms of communication – in order to reflect more clearly on the decisions made within their own work. As discussed in the previous chapter, it is useful for the designer to break down this activity into a series of interrelated stages, mapping on to the basic principles of field of study, project focus, methodology, technology and materials. The terminology used in the analysis of texts might be replicated in the description and construction of new material in order to qualify the intention of the designer more clearly: this can be seen as the shift from analysis to proposition.

Both qualitative and quantitative methods of design analysis might be necessary to conduct a thorough study of a piece of visual communication, either through decoding meanings in individual artefacts or through the collection and comparison of a range of related examples in order to evaluate design vocabularies selected as appropriate to a particular context or audience.

Denotation and Connotation

A particular word or a sign may have a literal meaning – this is called denotation, and it will also have a connotation or range of connotations.

Whilst denotation could almost be described as obvious or common sense in its literalness 'this is a photograph of two men talking and smiling', connotation refers to the range of cultural, social or personal interpretations of a sign, image or word (the two men in the photograph are brothers, in love, businessmen making a deal etc.). The way in which the photograph is printed, in soft focus or grainy and black and white, for example, will also generate interpretation and influence how the reader understands the image (see Materiality, page 160).

07 Birds of a Feather >>

These images (this page and opposite) are a range of signs that we recognize as denoting simple illustrations or silhouettes of a range of species within the biological genus *birds*.

However, they also have individual connotations. They may indicate a range of wild or domesticated animals, sources of food, rare or endangered species. They can also connote attributes such as speed, agility, stupidity, gracefulness or beauty, or they might symbolize flight, wildlife, nature or the environment. Alternatively, they could perhaps be a logotype for a particular corporation, or a set of symbols in a wildlife park enabling visitors to identify different animals to be seen within that environment.

Engaging with Visual Research

Visual research involves the designer in a broad range of activities, which contribute to the development of new design propositions in a number of ways. Firstly, the designer needs to understand the context within which the work is to be placed. This means that the range of materials already in existence within that context, the expectations of the target audience and the existing messages against which the work may be required to compete, all need to be taken into account.

Traditionally, design education has worked with contextual visual research at the level of materials gathering and the construction of 'mood boards' – rough layouts of a range of objects that relate to the message, giving an impression of the kind of 'feel' intended by the designer at the outset of the project. Some of these objects and visual elements might relate directly to the envisaged resolution, whilst others are incorporated to denote emotional aspirations and the underlying feelings that the product is intended to evoke. While this can be a useful exercise, particularly in relation to product design, advertising and marketing, graphic designers also need to develop a more sophisticated methodology for analysing a range of materials relevant to the proposed project.

Familiarity Counts

It is important for the designer to understand the range of visual languages and texts that already exist in the space that the proposed design will occupy. All audiences have expectations with which they interrogate and interact with visual messages – the aim of innovative design is to relate to these already familiar forms, and to extend the visual language used in new and exciting ways. This means that the form of the visual language carries meaning, before we even start to analyse the content of the message itself.

Open Texts

In the science or art of semiotics (see pages 92–93) denotation and connotation relate to the relationship between the signifier and the signified. The ways in which the connotative meaning of an image or sign are interpreted and understood by the 'reader' can be utilized as an analytical tool in the theorization of visual communication, and this method is often applied in relation to advertising and photography.

It also forms the basis of a useful strategy for the graphic designer in the construction of complex and engaging visual forms of communication. The understanding that visual messages can be treated as 'open texts' (see Text, page 30), and that their connotation is based upon the interpretation of the reader on the basis of their class, gender and education is known as 'polysemy', implying a multiple range of inferred meanings.

Anchorage and Relay

According to Barthes' theory of semiotics, there are two kinds of relationships between text and image: anchorage and relay. All images are polysemic – they are open to endless different readings and interpretations, implying an uncertainty of meanings. Because of this a linguistic message is often associated with a designed image, to guide its interpretation. In anchorage, the text 'anchors' the meaning of the image by naming the intended denotation, helping identification. The text directs the reader through the signifieds of the image (and thus towards a meaning chosen in advance).

In relay, the text and the image form a complementary relationship, and the text is intended to extend the initial reading of the image. Relay can often be found in comic strips and films.

As Marshall McLuhan succinctly put it in his 1967 manifesto, '...*the medium is the message*' – in other words, the ways in which we transmit and receive information have an important and direct effect on the content of that information and the ways in which that content is read and understood.

A colloquial way of making this point might be the phrase 'first impressions count' – our first encounter with a visual form gives an instant impression and level of expectation. Once we have seen the initial visual form, we anticipate at least a part of what we expect to see or hear next. This principle can be seen at work in contemporary film, for instance, where the director can move smoothly between shots and points of view in order to establish a narrative structure, or can jump cut to an unexpected frame in order to create elements of surprise, shock or humour.

As the linguistics theorist Roman Jakobson has stated, '...*the message does not and cannot supply all the meaning of the transaction, [and] ...a good deal of what is communicated derives from the context, the code, and the means of contact. Meaning, in short, resides in the total act of communication.*' Audience expectation is a key factor in the development of successful design solutions, and in the exploration of new forms of visual communication based on dialogue and audience interaction, themes which will be explored further in Chapter 5: Audience and Message.

The word 'theory' comes from the Greek word *theorema* meaning to review or to reflect. The dictionary defines theory as an explanation or system of anything: an exposition of the abstract principles of either a science or an art. Theory is a speculation on something rather than a practice.

David Crow
Visible Signs: An Introduction to Semiotics in the Visual Arts (2010)

Graphic Authorship

Contemporary graphic design is not always concerned with problem solving, or operating in relation to a client's brief. The exploration of a theme that interests the designer and the graphic response to that theme, which might enlighten and help to describe new visual languages that are applicable to other graphic solutions, is a core part of the research agenda. In effect, this places the design methodology itself as a central component of the design process. The testing and development of a visual vocabulary relevant to a specific context may then be further developed in order to address a number of problems within that same context. The resultant 'solutions' can then be drawn upon by the designer in relation to further practical and commercial work.

It is important at the outset, however, for the designer to establish a clear set of intentions for an individual project and a critical position, relative to the subject being explored, so as to be able to reflect on progress made and to test the resulting graphic messages against a set of stated criteria – in effect, replacing the client's brief with one of the designer's own creation. The resultant design propositions are then both a combination of the personal exploration of the subject and a nascent visual language that operates within a set of predetermined objectives.

Peirce's theories of semiotics stated that there are three principal kinds of signs used within visual, verbal or other forms of communication: icon, index and symbol.

Icon/Iconic

Icons are likenesses that convey the idea of the thing they represent by directly resembling or imitating the signified: looking, sounding, feeling, tasting or smelling like it – such as a portrait, a cartoon or a model.

Index/Indexical

Indices or indications convey information by their physical connection with the thing they represent. The signifier is not arbitrary but is directly connected in some way (physically or causally) to the signified – this link can be observed or inferred. Common examples include smoke indicating fire, 'signals' such as a telephone ringing or a doorbell, and 'pointers' such as a wayfinding mark or sign.

Symbol/Symbolic

Symbols are general signs that have become associated with their meanings by their use and convention, so that the relationship must be learnt. Examples include spoken and written language, punctuation marks, numbers, codes, flags and many graphic marks indicating notation or implied symbolic language to be interpreted and read by an audience familiar with the specific code.

08 Big and Bold >>

A roadside hoarding promoting the Big Texan Steakranch near Amarillo, Texas. Consider the range of connotations of this image: what kind of food might you expect to get at the Big Texan? What qualities might you expect a customer to encounter – including the service, menu, decor and furniture of the restaurant?

Key Concepts: Post-structuralism

Post-structuralism, in particular **deconstruction**, takes its starting point from the earlier ideas of structuralism proposed by Saussure and Peirce (see pages 92–93 and is significant as a theory or framework for considering the exploration of the opposition between speech and writing. The French philosopher Jacques Derrida challenges the idea that speech is regarded as more important than writing in his seminal work *Of Grammatology* (1998). Derrida states that all systems or structures have a centre – a point of origin – and that all systems are constructed from binary pairs that are in relation or opposition to each other.

The focus on speech versus writing is an example of a binary system: speech = presence (physical contact between speaker and listener) and writing = absence (the written word can be read without any need for contact in time or space – we can read the words of authors long since departed, or writers on the other side of the world). Speech, which is associated with presence, is traditionally favoured over writing and absence – Derrida terms this **logocentrism**. These oppositions (also referred to as antonyms) exist to define each other: GOOD-EVIL, for example, and that rather than operating separately they work together and are part of each other.

Post-structuralist ideas deny the distinction between the signifier and signified – signifiers are words that refer to other words and their meaning is determined by one word's difference from another. The meaning of an object (the signified) is not present in this sign itself but in its relation to other signs. Derrida terms this **'différance'**. The concepts of **denotation** and **connotation** (see pages 46–47) are useful in this context – every word or phrase has potentially two kinds of meaning: **primary**, literal meaning – **denotation** – and **secondary** meaning – **connotation**. This can be applied to all visual signs, and is a particularly powerful tool in the related fields of branding and advertising.

A magazine advertisement, for example, depicting an attractive, well-dressed couple in an expensive looking car may be a promotion for the clothes or jewellery they are wearing. The connotated meaning may suggest that purchasing one of these items is the key to achieving a happy life and a successful career, to own an expensive car and to have a relationship with an attractive partner. The context of this advertisement in a consumer or lifestyle magazine and our experiences and cultural background will have an impact on how we 'read' the image used and our relationship to its coded messages. The meaning of the representation and how we 'read' it is not fixed by is creator or author but is equally determined by the reader.

Case Study 04: **The English**

Gemma Dinham's project set out to explore the notion of *Englishness*, a term used to represent the amalgamation of a number of factors related to English national identity, culture and character. The interplay of these elements gives the English people a sense of who they are, or increasingly a sense of who they are not. Humour provides a cornerstone for English national identity, and by using this and appropriating visual clichés commonly associated with the culture, Dinham wanted to explore and parody aspects of national character as a vehicle for a better critical understanding of that cultural identity.

    The use of humour is prolific throughout almost all social interactions in English society. One of the central factors in the identification of the English sense of humour is the love of irony. Irony has many definitions, but perhaps the simplest of these is that it aims to make something understood by expressing its opposite. Sarcasm is a form of irony thought to be a particularly English brand of humour.

    Kate Fox, author of *Watching the English* (2005), further describes the English sense of humour as a mixture of 'armchair cynicism, ironic detachment and a squeamish distaste for sentimentality'. Humour is so omnipresent in English society that even the people themselves have become the focus for an ironic and self-referential form of mockery, and this long-standing tradition of self-deprecation and understatement is another feature strongly associated with the culture. To be able to joke about themselves requires a cultural group to closely observe their own society and behaviour, and English culture has a long history of critical and ironic reflection within the arts, literature and comedy.

The English Scheme

Many visual clichés come from commercial goods and packaging. Equally, many traditionally English brands have an emotive weight far above their intrinsic value as basic commodities. The consumer's attachment to these traditional products often has as much to do with the visual appeal of their packaging as the quality of their contents.

Following an extensive survey of a wide range of English traditional goods and brand identities, Dinham found a strong sense of national identity and familiarity in the packaging of food and common household products. She initially chose to parody these very strong visual styles through the incorporation of a range of common descriptions of national characteristics (opposite page).

IMPOTENT FURY
THE ENGLISH PERSPECTIVE

THE ENGLISH POLITENESS PERSPECTIVE

THE ENGLISH PERSPECTIVE

IMPOTENCE

THE ORIGINAL FORMULA

MADE FROM VIRGIN ENGLISH INHIBITION

50ml

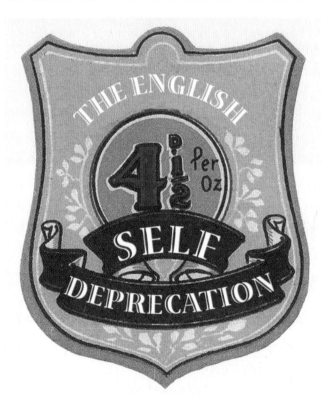

THE ENGLISH 4½ Per Oz SELF DEPRECATION

Case Study 04: The English

Whilst it would make sense to use irony as a method for revealing aspects of national character, it comes with risks: the problem with using irony is that people don't always notice it – to be ironic in the first place might require a culture in which irony is used regularly and understood. Dinham's research shows how deeply embedded humour is within the English national psyche, and how it exerts influence on almost every aspect of English life.

Dinham began her research by documenting a wide range of largely comic and humorous historical narratives related to national identity and character, giving rise to a number of caricatures and stereotypes that aim to represent the English people and their cultural identity. In order to visualize and parody these national character traits, the designer required a graphic vehicle through which to build a rhetorical commentary. Following an audit of English visual identity, it became apparent that many people have a particular nostalgic attachment to traditional English brands, and in particular their packaging. By parodying elements of this packaging and using their graphic style as a basis for the creation of new labels on existing products, Dinham was able to control these familiar associations and to build on their unspoken cultural connotations.

It is clear that for humour to work it has to be culturally specific both in terms of the situations or behaviours it refers to, and also in the type of humour used to deliver the amusement. English culture relies heavily on irony and self-deprecation, and Dinham's final 'products' simply turn the mirror back onto the culture itself – employing phrases associated with the stereotypical national character and using them as labels on her range of fictitious alcoholic drinks.

Bottled Up
Humour is a term that usually refers to some absurdity in human nature or conduct which causes amusement and sometimes laughter. It is found in every culture across the globe, and often relies on subtle social observations and commentary within each specific society to work – it can be self-reflective and referential, understood within the cultural group but not necessarily outside of it. For this reason, specific types of culturally focused humour may or may not translate more widely across other cultures.

As the British broadcaster and journalist Jeremy Paxman has asked, '…does any other society put such a premium upon having a sense of humour?' Humour is central to the English way of life. It is found in almost every social situation, and is integral to the national sense of identity and the shared understanding of English culture and values.

Dinham progressed her ironic product labelling to focus on a more specific range of brands and types of goods. She chose to work with a selection of generic alcohol products and packages, in order to pass comment on the national association with a number of different types of alcohol consumption, and the relationship between social etiquette, class, mannerisms and alcoholic drinks.

These packages were stylized as direct parodies of existing graphic conventions, such as the labelling and generic style of real ales and traditional beers (opposite page).

Class Character

In order to make the 'products' appear as realistic as possible, the designer chose to develop additional product labelling, including details of nutritional information, volume, ingredients, instructions for storage or consumption and other ephemeral elements typically found on each product. This additional space for textual information was utilized to further develop her approach to satirizing national character. It could also be more carefully fine-tuned toward the stereotypical drinker of each category of alcohol product, and the class associations of those types of individuals (above and right).

To keep the project well within the realms of Englishness, Dinham chose drinks that were either traditionally thought to be closely associated or that had gained widespread popularity within the culture and had therefore entered the fabric of contemporary English society. For example lager, although not traditional to England like ale, became very popular from the 1960s onwards, and is now the most widely consumed alcoholic beverage in the country. The final range of 'products' included packaging for real ale, white wine, cheap cider, strong lager and gin (next page).

ENGLISH

EST. 1845

CYNICISM

CRISP, DRY & SARCASTIC

BREWED FROM ENGLAND'S
FINEST

4.2% VOLUME

ENGLISH

EST. 1979

POLITENESS

Traditionally bottle fermented
with subtle notes of contempt

12% VOLUME

EN

ES

IMPO

Scarcel

FOR AN IN

SERVE OVE

Case Study 05: **An Inventory of Loss**

Museums collect and display artefacts in order to educate and inform their visitors, and to preserve important cultural achievements of the past and present. Neil Mabbs' project focuses on a range of items that are not 'treasured' – the used and rejected objects found in charity shops and junk stores. The work explores the idea that in every store, every object is a potential 'artefact', and that everything has significance. The designer describes An Inventory of Loss as '…*a visual inventory of rejected objects found in charity shops, the museums of the everyday life of the past, where things that have lost their former use value now search for a new one.*' He attempted, through a series of books, to deconstruct what he terms '*the semiotics of the forlorn*': the semiotic structure of abandoned objects found in charity shops and car boot sales, the 'white elephant goods' that have outlived their usefulness to the person who owns

them. Drawing on the ordinary and everyday, his work explores the relationship between us and the transient nature of objects we surround ourselves with.

Mabbs attempted to study the changing fortunes of a range of items and to document their journey from useful or treasured artefacts to abandoned and hopeless objects. He aimed to explore how these objects lose their appeal, how they go out of fashion or stop working, and how they lose their social or cultural significance and their personal associations. Drawing on theories of the aesthetic, functional and cultural value of objects, Mabbs' work visually reflects what Thomas Seelig and Urs Stahel describe in their photographic history of designed objects, *The Ecstasy of Things* (2008), as; '…*these objects, no longer of any use, no longer desired, become aging divas, withered and hoarse, still waiting for one last grand performance – at the jumble sale or charity shop.*'

Loss of Form

Mabbs produced a set of four final books, each exploring a different theme and a related practical design method. Following on from his initial typology of the complete archive of visual material collected, *Book #1: Inventory of Everything*, *Book #2: Loss of Form* alludes to scientific schemes for the purpose of comparative study and, in the words of the designer '…*attempts to evoke a more fetishistic, exotic*

response to the ordinary objects documented.'

Loss of Form sets out to ask the question of whether what we see is a function of what we know. When confronted with something we do not understand, in an attempt to find our way through the visual chaos, forms have to be found to provide order, categories and types have to be created. *Loss of Form* documents a series of wrapped

objects bought from charity shops that defy or undermine a language of description by making it impossible to name, label or classify the object (opposite page). The irregularity of form shatters our understanding of common names, destroying the syntax with which we construct meaning: these 'things' have no clear reference or context through which they can be articulated as objects.

Within this book, the designer considered it of secondary importance whether we know which object resided where, when and where it was manufactured, how big it is, of what materials it is made. This information, although included, is relegated to an index at the back of the book.

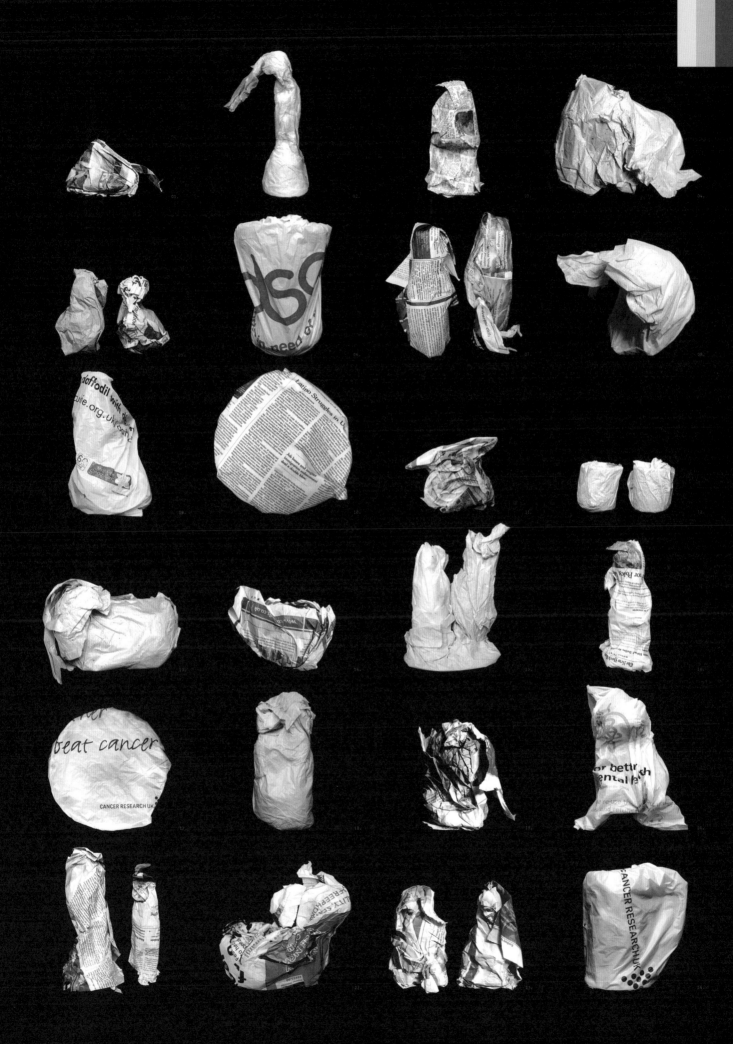

Case Study 05: An Inventory of Loss

The Semiotics of Value

One central aim of An Inventory of Loss is to lead the viewer beyond the objects to consider their provenance, or sources and lineages of ownership, as well as the ways in which collecting has served as a central base for knowledge in the West. Mabbs also referenced Rubbish Theory (see pages 124–125) – the creation and destruction of value attributed to these objects, and their transition from desirable items to the detritus of modern life. He followed several alternative routes of enquiry, documenting his findings through a variety of graphic design methods and processes, from a simple photographic typology of objects and source locations to a number of practical methods that attempted to reflect values related to form, cost or value, age and time. The work also relates closely to a range of theories of the photographic image – Mabbs used photography as a working process throughout his research, and he was particularly interested in the reading of those photographs, as images of objects, rather than the objects themselves.

Four final books were produced, charting the different routes of enquiry and graphic design methods employed. *Book #1: Inventory of Everything* shows the entire database of photographs as a series of typologies, *Book #2: Loss of Form* explores the reading of the objects as forms without content or context, *Book #3: Loss of Order* charts the perceived relationship between objects randomly placed together in sales boxes, and *Book #4: Loss of Nostalgia* focuses on a particular subset of items; ornaments commemorating visits to tourist or holiday destinations. Graphic design methods were utilized to not only present the information gathered, but to reveal aspects of the designer's research process through their material or visual form.

Inventory of Everything

A plastic doll, a glass vase, a ceramic pig, a hairdryer, jigsaw puzzles, a picture in a frame, a pair of sunglasses – these are all incongruous objects. But what do they have in common? This at least: they are all signs.

When we walk into a charity shop or visit a car-boot sale we encounter these objects and, without realizing, we 'read' them.

As members of the same culture we share these 'readings', thus interpreting the world in roughly the same way. Broadly speaking, they must share the same 'cultural codes'. Similarly, in order to communicate these meanings to other people, the participants in any meaningful exchange must also be able to use the same linguistic codes – they must broadly 'speak the same language'.

An object is defined as: anything that is visible or tangible and is relatively stable in form; a thing, person, or matter to which thought or action is directed. In short, an object is 'something', and the things that we commonly call objects usually reflect mass manufacturing – the notion of the object reproduced in thousands of examples, in millions of copies. Ordinarily, we define these objects as having a function, a utility, a purpose, and this is how we relate to them, as instruments.

Mabbs' extensive photographic documentary of objects for sale in charity shops, junk shops and car-boot sales, formed the basis of a typology within his first book in the series, *Book #1: Inventory of Everything* (opposite page).

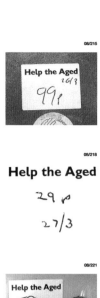
Help the Aged

08/215 08/216 08/217 08/239 08/240 08/241

08/218 08/219 08/220 08/242 08/243 08/244

08/221 08/222 08/223 08/245 08/246 08/247

08/224 08/225 08/226 08/248 08/249 08/250

08/284 08/285 08/286 08/061 08/062 08/063

08/287 08/288 08/289 08/064 08/065 08/066

08/290 08/291 08/292 08/067 08/068 08/069

08/293 08/294 08/295 08/070 08/071 08/072

Object Relations

When a collection of objects are put together, meaning is no longer produced from any single object, but from the assemblage of objects. Whether these are ornaments and furniture in a room or a collection of objects on a shelf in a charity shop, they are linked by a single form of connection: the simple juxtaposition of elements. Roland Barthes refers to this kind of juxtaposition as 'parataxis'.

However, while some elements are intended to be displayed adjacent to one another – as in an interior design, or a formal display in a museum or shop, for instance – the signifieds of the system of objects assembled in charity shops and at car-boot sales are harder to decipher, as their arrangement may be accidental. The signifieds of such objects depend not so much on the arranger of these objects, the emitter of the message, but on

the receiver, the reader of these objects. And as each of us has several ways of reading, depending on the kinds of knowledge of culture we possess, when facing a collection of these ephemeral objects, many readings of meaning are possible.

Archival photography is typically marked by directness, frontality, regularity and an apparent lack of artifice or artistry. This mode of

photography enables comparative readings of types: it creates visual systems of classification, of likeness and difference. Mabbs developed a highly systematic approach to the documentation of the various found objects under investigation, formally photographing individual items from two opposing aspects (opposite top), and cataloguing collections of objects by date and location, alongside observed object groupings (opposite bottom).

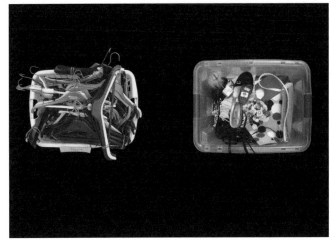

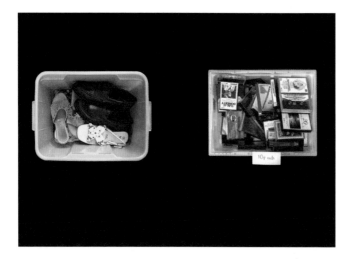 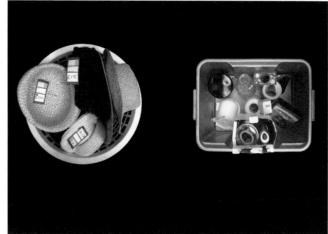

Still Out of Order

Book #3: Loss of Order explores a number of accidental and unusual juxtapositions of unrelated objects, and the familiar yet disconcerting effect that occurs when we link together things or objects that have no or little relation to each other. The book is a collection of photographs of items found within forty 'tubs of tat' (reduced items) found for sale in charity shops (above and opposite page). The colloquial term 'tat' is defined as *'tastelessness by virtue of being cheap and vulgar: cheapness'* (www.dictionary.com).

In his introduction to the book, Mabbs states that *'…there is a stubbornness to these objects, a resistance to our need to classify and order them.'* The uniqueness of each object stresses its isolation to those around it, and emphasizes the loss of the context within which is it normally placed. The designer's approach aimed to overlap photographic practice with taxonomic methods, exploring the subtle relationship between subjective aesthetic and objective document. The work tries to make effective use of photography's essential capacity to describe and to present, with varying degrees of directness and complexity, visual evidence drawn from the real world. The work explores the rhetoric of the photograph as scientific evidence and combines the techniques of display and labelling, notes, field photographs and ephemera.

Was | Now

Nostalgia

Book #4: Loss of Nostalgia continues to explore what Mabbs terms the marginal object, in this case as a series of cyanotypes produced to record a collection of 21 tourist souvenirs found in charity shops. The book asks us to consider the layers of time and experience embedded within these objects, and to reflect upon the structures that shape everyday life. These layers of time implicate different histories: the personal histories of the objects on the shelves and their former owners.

The cyanotype process for making prints was invented by the astronomer Sir John Herschel in 1842 and involves paper treated with iron salt solution on which the object or negative to be produced is placed and left in the sun. After a short time (around two to eight minutes), an impression of the object is seen on a brilliant blue or cyan background. Although all of the images in this collection contain strikingly contemporary objects, the process gives them a Victorian feel.

The souvenir is an object arising out of the necessarily insatiable demands of nostalgia. The tourist souvenirs that we collect are representations of things done, seen and admired. All this ephemera can be brought under the heading of 'markers' of personal experiences or events. The final book is a collection of photographs of rejected 'markers' and uses exposure time as a variable for their visual representation (above and opposite page bottom). Calculations factored the exposure of each object within the cyanotype process against the length of time that it had been on display in the charity shop (opposite page top).

Cyanotype tests

Conclusion.
don't use someset → pale imaging faded.
fabriano absorbs cyanotype →
results in deeper blue image.

Date: 28/7 **Weather:** ☁/70° **Time of day:** 11:00 — 3:00

Object (negative)	Neg no./type	Paper	Exp Time (MINS)	Method application / no. of coats.	Neg no./ type	Paper	Exp Time (MINS).	Method
Musical lady	1 & LASERt	Somerset	full sun 10 mins	old sensitizer/rod — 1 coat	2. Laser	Fabriano	full sun 5	old / rod / 1
Ardeche bowl	3. laser	Somerset	full sun 10	new / rod / 1	4. Laser	somerset	full sun 5	new / rod / 2 coats
Verona Arena	5. laser	Fabriano	full sun 5	new / brush / 1	(22) SPANISH DOLLS. inkjet LANGTON	12 sun.	rod 1.
Big Ben bell	6. allaser inkjet.	FAB 5.	sun th 5	new / rod / 2 1	7. laser	FAB 5.	sun 7.	new/rod / 2
Doll in box	11. abser	Fabriano	sun 7.	new / rod / 1.	(21) SPANISH MN.	object.	sun 12 mins	brush 1.
Drachen German mug	8. laser	Fabriano	sun 5.	rod / new / 1	9. Voba inkjet	somerset	sun 6	new / rod / 1.
Southsea seagull	12. laser inkjet	Somerset.	cloudy 6.	new / rod / 2.	13. inkjet	somerset.	cloudy 8	new / rod / 1.
Wangth Snow Storm Holland	②inkjet	FABRIANO ARTISTICO 200 gsn	full sun 2.5	rod / old / 1	④ inkjet	full sun 1 min	⑥ inkjet 30-40 secs full sun
Clockwork monkey (full)	① inkjet	" "	" "	rod / old / 1.	③ inkjet	full sun 1 min	⑤ inkjet 30-40 secs full sun
Monkey (close-up)	23 SEAGULL inkjet / LANGTON	2½ sun	rod / 1.	15 Monkey / inkjet	fabriano 200 gsm	4 mins sun	rod / 1.
Donkey & cart	inkjet	FAB 5.	cloudy 10	new / rod / 1.	17 monkey / inkjet	lot 200	6½ sun.	" ..
Barcelona plate Turkey clock	inkjet	lot 200 gsm	cloudy	2	old / old	24 SPANISH DOLLS	inkjet LANGTON	1½ sun.	rod / 2.
Italian Man Italian Gondola	⑧ inkjet	lot 200 gsm	cloudy	2	old / old.	27 SEAGULL	LANGTON	2½ sun	rod / 1
Jersey Maid PARIS HANKY	① inkjet	full sun 1 min FAB 200 gsm	⑩ → hanky Langton 3 mins	⑪ hanky - Langton - 5 mins	⑫ — 10 mins

Readings chart → | neg no | type | paper | method no. of coats / application | exp. time | result poor / faded etc.

Key Concepts: Rubbish Theory

First proposed by Michael Thompson in his book of the same name (1979), **Rubbish Theory** relates to **the creation and destruction of value** within man-made objects, cultural artefacts and ideas. As a social scientist, Thompson became interested in the ways in which objects carry an economic or cultural value, which diminishes over time, to the point where they become redundant and worthless. However, Thompson noted that some objects then begin to accrue value once more as time goes on – such as antiques, vintage cars and Georgian terraced houses.

Objects can then make the journey from a region Thompson describes as **transient** (value decreasing), through **rubbish** (no value) to **durable** (value increasing). When this idea is applied to a house, for example, we can see that a building may have an initially high value, dependent on status, cost and function, which may decrease over time in relation to an expected lifespan, after which it may have little or no residual value and could be demolished to make way for a new building in its place. However, although this obsolescence tends to happen with certain kinds of property (low-cost housing built in the 1960s, for example), it is not the case with Georgian or Victorian English town houses, which the estate agent terms 'period properties', and which are then highly desirable, and expensive. Durability is, thus, socially constructed.

The actions of an individual relate to his or her own **world view** – the way in which he or she perceives the world, based on cultural heritage, education and experience – and Thompson's theory attempts to draw our attention to the ways in which our understanding of objects is socially constructed and understood. He goes further in refuting the ideals of **transaction theory**, whereby an agreement is implied between individuals transacting over a valued object, based on their range of shared assumptions.

Although different, these assumptions are harmonized over time due to each individual adapting their approach and world view in order to achieve better results in their next transaction – which leads to the homogeneous world view (or shared cultural values) of a social group or community. Thompson argues that this process is, by definition, static in its exclusion of the range of external influences on the individuals involved, and the fact that their perception of the results of their actions may be different from reality. These ideas are useful to the producers of transient and durable objects – such as graphic designers – in helping to describe the complex relationship between the cultural artefact and its perceived value or use.

Exercises: The Practice of Theory

Objective

This exercise explores how theoretical ideas can be employed to underpin design projects and design practice in general. Theory in itself has no practical application but is a useful tool for understanding. When used within design activity it becomes part of a more strategic approach to design – what the American educator and designer Thomas Ockerse has called *'principles in action'*. This exercise builds upon the notion of visual rhetoric – in large part based on the understanding that the effective communication of an idea is closely linked to the act of persuasion.

Rhetoric traditionally encompasses a range of figures of speech, including irony, antithesis, metonymy, synecdoche, pun, metaphor, personification and hyperbole, some of which may be utilized by the designer within visual strategies (see pages 72–73).

Gui Bonsiepe has written that 'pure' information exists for the designer only in abstraction. As soon as he or she begins to give it concrete shape, a process of rhetorical infiltration begins.

Part 1: Visual Irony and Pun

You are asked to explore how using visual irony means you can take an existing sign – a logo, picture or visual device – and change its meaning. A good example of this can be seen in the détournement* of the logos and visual identities of multinational corporations for example by organizations such as Adbusters and those 'culture jammers' opposed to the perceived values and activities of these companies.

Choose a company, product or informational sign, then begin to explore how you are able to make something that is familiar and that, to a large extent is

Key Texts

Barthes, R. (1993) *Image – Music – Text*. Fontana Books.

Berger, J. (2008) *Ways of Seeing*. London: Penguin Classics.

Crow, D. (2006) *Left to Right: The Cultural Shift from Words to Pictures*. Worthing: AVA Publishing SA.

Crow, D. (2010) *Visible Signs: An Introduction to Semiotics*, 2nd edition. Worthing: AVA Publishing SA.

Gage, J. (2000) *Colour and Meaning: Art, Science and Symbolism*. London: Thames and Hudson.

Kress, G. R. and Van Leeuwen, T. (1996) *Reading Images: The Grammar of Visual Design*. London and New York: Routledge.

Lupton, E., Abbott Miller, J. (1996) *Design Writing Research: Writing on Graphic Design*. London: Phaidon.

Poynor, R. (2003) *No More Rules: Graphic Design and Postmodernism*. London: Laurence King Publishing.

not noticed, say something different or oppositional. This could be achieved by altering one or some of its key attributes; colour, typeface, symbol or image for example, or by changing the context or location of the sign/media. It is important that you are careful in your selection of the 'original' media so that it is one that an audience will be familiar with in order for them to be able to appreciate its new oppositional reading. This process can also be explained by Semiotics (see pages 92–93) – the relationship between what is seen and the mental concept it produces – and the notion of Connotation and Denotation (see pages 46–47).

Part 2: Metaphor

You are asked to select a film or novel and produce a poster that explores how its meaning(s) or narrative ideas can be represented through the use of a visual device or series of visual items. A visual metaphor can be understood to work in a similar way to the processes at work in Part 1 of this exercise: for it to work effectively it has to build upon the understanding an audience already possesses.

Try to select a film or novel that is well known – a classic. Initially you should explore the obvious metaphors; for example *Romeo and Juliet* could be easily understood by the use of symbols that stand for love. You should build upon this foundation to further develop your ideas to a more sophisticated level. How can other narrative subtexts be illustrated in a metaphorical manner? What can be said visually that makes a stronger and more abstract connection with the minds of the audience and their existing knowledge of the film or book? Can you update the meaning by using a contemporary metaphor or idea, for example?

* Détournement
A technique devised in the 1950s by the Situationist International and intended as an act that turned the messages and intentions of capitalism in on itself.

It is interesting to note that this process can also be seen at work in the manner in which mainstream culture, and in particular media, can take symbols of opposition or subversion and appropriate them into commodities or make them 'safe' – this process was termed 'recuperation' by the Situationists (see page 139).

5. Audience and Message

The relationship between designer, audience and message, and the principles of communication

Receiving End

Building on the communication theory precepts outlined in Chapter 3: Analysis and Proposition, this chapter further investigates the relationship between designer, audience and message, and considers alternative strategies for communicating through both direct and indirect means. The production of design within a social, cultural and political context is further explored, placing both the designer and the audience as co-participants within predefined frameworks.

Any general definition of graphic design and its intentions cannot fail to make reference to communication and audience. In this regard, graphic designers could develop a vocabulary for describing and understanding their working methods through the language and theory of communication studies. Although a separate discipline with a much broader remit than graphic design, communication studies incorporates a series of useful analytical and descriptive methodologies, which relate strongly to graphic and visual communication.

Are You Receiving Me?

Two schools of thought exist within communication theory, the first of which might be described as the 'process school' – an approach to the subject that is concerned with the actual processes of communication. This school highlights the channels and media through which messages are transmitted and by which senders and receivers encode and decode, in particular the setting up of a model of analysis that is concerned with matters of efficiency and accuracy.

If the process of communication creates a different effect from that which is intended by the transmitter, and this in turn leads to a misreading or aberrant interpretation, then that reveals a breakdown in transmission, a flawed system or channel. This

World View
A term adopted from a translation of the German word *Weltanschauung*, world view refers to the overall perspective from which an individual or group sees and interprets the world around them.

It can also be used to describe a collection of beliefs about the world held by an individual or a group. These belief systems are often represented through myths, ceremonies, patterns of social behaviour and the set of shared general values held by a social or cultural group.

school of thought envisages a message as that which is transmitted by the communication process (and maintains that intention is a crucial factor in deciding what constitutes a message).

By contrast, the 'semiotic school' is concerned with the message as a construction of signs which, through interaction with receivers, produces meaning. This school of thought views communication as an agent in the construction and exchange of meaning: by using terms like signification (related to the constituent parts of a message), it does not consider misunderstandings to be necessarily evidence of communication failure. Advocates for this model argue that a differing interpretation within the process of communication would validate a position more concerned with the plurality and unstable nature of messages, and with their perception of an audience dependent on culture and context.

Post/Modernity

The approaches of these two schools of thought could also be applied to what are often described as the modernist and postmodernist positions within current graphic design practice and theory. The 'process school' of graphic design – modernity and its legacy – is motivated by notions of universality, rationality, the clarity of communication through legibility, neutrality and the grid. This arguably utopian world view, based on form and functionality and a homogeneous process, could be characterized as dealing with absolutes within communication.

By contrast, what might be called postmodern approaches to graphic design embrace and promulgate the view of design and visual communication as an important component in the plurality of contemporary culture, and seek to emphasize its role in constructing a matrix of interpretation.

Post-structuralism

A body of theory relating to the distinctions between speech and writing. The French philosopher Jacques Derrida, in his seminal work *Of Grammatology* (1998), challenged the idea that speech is more important than writing. Derrida stated that all systems or structures have a centre – a point of origin – and that all systems are constructed from binary pairs that are in relation or opposition to each other.

Deconstruction

The term deconstruction denotes a particular kind of practice in reading, and a mode of analytical critical enquiry. It is a theory of reading that aims to expose and undermine the logic of opposition within texts (both written and visual).

This critical analysis sets out to question the priority of things that are set up as original, natural, or self-evident. Deconstructive readings are often part of a broader form of interpretation based on a firm critical position (for instance feminist, new historicist or Marxist critique). As such, they are often used to destabilize the range of inherent hierarchical oppositions in the text (between male and female, elite and popular culture, economic class, etc.). For further reading, see Key Concepts: Post-structuralism, page 104.

Receiving End

Less concerned with broad bands of communication, this approach to the construction and reading of visual communication addresses specific and focused, and often smaller, communities and groups, which might be described in social, economic, or geographic terms.

The recognition that designed objects exist within a social structure, and are read by their receivers from a particular cultural perspective and subjective world view, is central to an understanding of audience-specific graphic design. While certain forms of graphic design may offer some claim to the modernist objectives of universality and mass communication, much contemporary design work operates within more limited and specific boundaries. As such, a sense of familiarity with the graphic languages already understood by the target audience is crucial to the development of effective design solutions. Both qualitative and quantitative

approaches are useful here, in the collection and analysis of a range of visual material operating within the same space as the intended message.

A qualitative analysis of existing artefacts and visual solutions, through the semiotic principles of connotation and denotation discussed in Chapter 2: Design Literacy, can help the designer to interrogate the underlying principles within effective visual messages targeting the same audience. Meanwhile, quantitative methods for reviewing and analysing a broad range of objects in the same space, and gathering feedback from focus or survey groups, can help to create a bigger picture of the range of cultural readings and messages already in place. Knowledge of existing material with which the proposed message will compete is crucial to the development of a successful design solution.

Social

Relating to human society and its members, this term is used to describe the context within which humans live together in communities or organized groups. In relation to public forms of visual communication and graphic design aimed at a broad audience demographic, social space is the realm in which interaction and communication generally takes place between individuals.

Cultural

In his seminal dictionary of terms used in philosophy and cultural studies, *Keywords* (1976), Raymond Williams noted that '…*culture is one of the two or three most complicated words in the English language.*'

The noun 'culture' is often used to describe a particular society at a particular time and place, together with the attitudes and behaviour that are characteristic of a particular

social group or organization (often within a contemporaneous context). However, the term is extremely broad and can refer to a wide number of parallel and distinct themes, often interrelated with a range of social values and conventions.

The adjective 'cultural' refers to the tastes in art and manners that are favoured by a social group, often the social elite within a wider society. As

such the term can be interpreted as pejorative, describing a hierarchical position within a value system.

Distant Relatives

It is also important to consider the relationship between designer and client, and between client and audience, as well as that between designer, designed object and audience. It should be noted that the designer may play only one part within the creative team involved in a project whose members may range from marketing consultants to copywriters, programmers and manufacturers.

This is an area that is sometimes overlooked but the relationship and process of negotiation between client and designer is a key development in the definition of the brief itself. Sometimes, the client may be unsure of the best way to target a particular audience, or may be unclear as to the specific intentions of the message itself which may be necessary to achieve a desired goal. In this case, the designer can play a central role in revising and defining the brief in order to address specific needs and provide a practical solution for the client.

Within commercial practice, the need for this kind of negotiation may mark the distinction between the context-definition and context-experiment areas of research mentioned earlier (see page 59). Context-definition may be appropriate where the client has a good knowledge of their market or audience, and the brief might reflect this by being strongly prescriptive in the range of activities expected of the designer.

Where the client is unsure of the specific problem to be addressed, the context experiment model could help to refine the project. In this case, the designer's initial research can help to inform the direction that the project will take, and the process of negotiation between client and designer is foregrounded.

Design is not an abstract theoretical discipline – it produces tangible artefacts, expresses social priorities and carries cultural values. Exactly whose priorities and values is at the core of the debate.

Andrew Howard
'A New Kind of Dialogue' in *Adbusters: Design Anarchy* issue (2001)

The Construction of Meaning

Contextual research conducted by the graphic designer can both inform the client and focus the project, and will also provide a strong base on which to develop an appropriate and useful solution. It is also important to consider the role the audience themselves play in the construction of meaning within the context of visual communication.

Some designers have attempted to break with the traditions of the transmitter-receiver model of visual communication, either through more consultative approaches to the design itself (particularly in areas such as service design and transformation design), or in the creation of graphic design outcomes that offer a more open space for 'dialogue' and interpretation to take place.

Although the notion of the passive receiver of a message has been questioned within communication and language studies for many years now, it remains a fundamental principle within graphic design, both in the profession and within the academy. Through the creation of more fluid and 'open' visual messages, the designer can attempt to engage the reader in a dialogue, to empower the receiver in the construction of meaning from within a message. By breaking the hierarchy implicit in the transmission of messages, this model could also help to critique the values underpinning the message itself as well as the medium through which it is transmitted, graphic design. Experiments in this field include the wide range of visual responses to the theories of post-structuralism and deconstruction (see pages 104–105), particularly those conducted at the Cranbrook Academy of Art in the US during the mid-1990s, together with the 'reflexive' work of politically active designers such as Jan van Toorn in the Netherlands.

Audience

A group of spectators or listeners at a concert or a play, or the people reached by a book, film, radio or television programme, for instance. The audience for a graphic design product is usually clearly defined by the client or, following a period of primary research, by the designer in consultation with the client.

The term 'audiencing' refers to the ways in which readers interpret and understand texts. Surveys of audience reading are often based on methods adopted from qualitative social science, such as interviews and ethnographic studies, together with quantitative methods based on statistical analysis.

However, one further model for graphic designers to consider is the reflective critical interpretation of images, which can often include a personal deconstruction of existing work or a critical reflection on work being undertaken by the designer. Through this analysis of design methods, the designer can become more expert in the range of forms and approaches suitable for a particular context or audience.

09 The Black Mailbox >>
Located on Highway 375, also known as the Extraterrestrial Highway, in the Nevada desert, close to the controversial US military airbase at Area 51, this mailbox has become a primary destination for UFO spotters. The original black box was sold to a UFO collector and replaced with a reinforced steel white box some years ago, but the name remains unchanged.

SEND

RECEIVE

Two-way Communication

Experiments that relate directly to communication theory can be a useful tool for graphic designers in charting alternative views of the function and purpose of visual communication – in particular those giving a greater emphasis to the receiver of the message. This way of thinking about design and communication is useful, as it allows the designer to view the reader as an active, rather than passive, participant in the process. The construction and interpretation of the message, focused in this way as an activity centred on the world view, social and cultural background of the receiver, can lead to a more engaged, and therefore more effective, form of communication.

Of course, this is relevant within both academic and commercial arenas: even where a commercial project attempts to target a particular market sector, an appreciation of the audience within that environment is crucial to a successful resolution.

This is essential in relation to branding and identity design, where audience engagement and response is crucial to the success and longevity of the graphic message. Brand loyalty is based on far more than the graphic identity of a producer, of course, but once an audience has 'bought into' the range of feelings promoted within an identity, the designer can make subtle and incremental adjustments in order to maintain a sense of exclusivity or inside knowledge in the mind of the loyal customer.

Within the allied fields of marketing and advertising, audience analysis and demographic studies are seen as key areas of research in the development of a project or campaign. This aspect of the creative process has become increasingly important in those areas of graphic design that attempt to address specific groups of people, such as editorial and information design, and in graphic design

Parody

A parody is a work created in order to mock, pass comment on, or make fun of an original work, its subject, author, style, or some other target, by means of humorous, satirical or ironic imitation. The term stems from literature, but can be seen widely within areas of graphic design, such as activist and protest graphics (blending with satirical approaches in the latter), as well as the fields of advertising and entertainment.

Pastiche

A pastiche is an imitation of an original earlier work, though with a different intention from a parody, which seeks to refer in itself to the audience's familiarity with the original. A pastiche may imply a generally light-hearted stylistic imitation, which although humorous is usually respectful, but it may also be seen as a less valuable 'copy' without any clear or intended reference to the original work.

Satire

Satire is often strictly defined as a literary technique of writing which principally ridicules its subject often with the intention of provoking a change or reaction. More recently it has been used within graphic design, comedy, performance and film to great effect. Humour is often used to aid the satirical position, with approaches adopting the widespread use of ridicule, irony and sarcasm.

targeted at audiences in areas of popular culture, such as fashion and popular music.

Audience-centred graphic design, then, covers a broad range of activities, from specific communication intended for a tightly defined target group of readers or market, to attempts at empowering the receiver of the message through the employment of visual devices that reveal and display the medium itself, and hence highlight the communication process at work. A substantial body of work relating to audiencing and reception exists within television studies and film theory, but little work has been done in this area with regard to graphic design and the wider fields of visual communication. An examination of the ways in which readers interpret visual messages in printed form, within motion graphics on screen or via interactive displays could prove beneficial to designers *and* cultural theorists.

Given that graphic design is largely based on very clear and specific intentions with regard to the content and context of a message, this would appear to be an area rich in potential for further study.

Détournement

A term devised by the Situationist International, an art-based protest group active during the mid- to late-1960s in France and surrounding countries, *détournement* describes the *turning around* of power structures within images and other forms of mass communication, through appropriation and satirical intervention. The original intention of détournement was to break what the situationists saw as the *Spectacle*, the invisible codes and conventions of society and culture, which they believed supported and reinforced dominant ideological power structures and hegemonies.

The strategy was later adopted by notable designers in the mid-1970s, such as Jamie Reid, whose sleeve designs and posters for punk group the Sex Pistols refined the approach within the context of abrasive, agitational and politically confrontational graphic design. As a graphic language of protest and subversion, this style has continued to resonate to this day.

Case Study 06: **Hybrid Novels**

Stories are an important aspect of culture. Many works of art, and most works of literature, tell stories, and storytelling was probably one of the earliest forms of human communication. At a time in which the tradition of reading physical books is becoming outmoded and the sale of e-books is rapidly increasing, designer Alberto Hernández felt that the use of visual devices in books that encourage us to read them in our own hands and feel the experience of engaging with a physical artefact could become increasingly important.

The designer's intention in this project was to try – by adding playful graphic devices to a chosen novel – to engage readers in a more dynamic narrative experience, to help them understand the story more easily, and to give the printed page a multidimensional visual surface. He was not only interested in the story the author creates for readers, but in the story readers create in their minds within a particular novel.

By intervening in the narrative of a chosen novel, through a range of graphic techniques and devices, he set out to involve readers in new ways and help them to understand the narrative more easily and in what he saw as a more satisfyingly experiential manner. Hernández considered various possibilities of subject text, before settling on *The Strange Case of Dr Jekyll and Mr Hyde*, written by the Scottish author Robert Louis Stevenson and first published in 1886. The main reason for this choice was the unusual way in which its narrative was presented as a dossier of witness statements to describe a series of events.

According to Hernández' definition a hybrid novel is not a children's book, graphic novel/comic or gift book, but a book where written text and graphic devices, such as illustration, photography, information graphics or typographic treatments may intervene to hold a reader's interest, adding a sense of interaction.

Victorian Imagery

Hernández wanted his hybrid novel to reflect a range of visual styles and images stemming from the period of its original publication in the late Victorian era. He visited a number of places related to the story, including Hampstead cemetery, which holds many Victorian tombs; St Pancras Old Church, where incidents of tomb robbery and body snatching took place in the Victorian era; the

Hunterian Museum, since it is said that the house where Dr Jekyll lives in the story is based on Dr Hunter's house on the same site; and the Freud museum, as Freud's ideas in regard to psychoanalysis and unconsciousness are a core theme throughout the original text.

In addition, Hernández visited the V&A Museum, the British Library and the Wellcome collection in order to gather source information

and visual material from Victorian books and scientific research. Although he wanted a Victorian 'feel' to the final book, the designer did not constrain his collection of graphic ephemera purely to a rigid historical context, utilizing other examples of medical imagery and advertising (opposite top and bottom right), together with his own photography (opposite bottom left) in order to stress a range of themes within the text.

Following this visual audit of secondary material, an extensive body of visual information from advertising to biological research was collated to be used within the hybrid novel, and a number of alternative graphic approaches were investigated in order to develop the final visual style.

Case Study 06: Hybrid Novels

As such, the hybrid novel is a book that demands to be handled and experienced, requiring action on the part of the reader.

Stevenson's story of Dr Jekyll and Mr Hyde is about duality and split personality, but it also contains various secondary ideas relating to psychoanalysis and sexuality, evolutionary anthropology, criminology, phrenology, science, religion and the realm of dreams. The designer set out to incorporate these subtexts within the design of the hybrid novel, drawing on contemporaneous Victorian imagery, publications and bodies of knowledge for material. The remediated book is a compendium of elements relating to dualism, asymmetry and combinations, utilizing different typefaces, paper stocks and colour palettes throughout in order to visualize the concept.

Two completely different typefaces were used to set the text of the story: New Caledonia, which has elements of the Scotch Roman typeface, one of the most widely used book types in Victorian times, and Grotesque, one of the earliest sans serif typefaces, which was used to set the title and contents pages. These two types maintain a Victorian flavour to the remediation, but also retain the element of duality.

A wide range of paper was employed, from Bible paper to newsprint, highly textured and even glossy paper. In addition, a variety of peach and salmon colours was used, as a link to the subtext of homosexuality in the novel. Having a variety of different colours also gives the remediation a more unsettling feeling and suggests the idea that there are different documents contained within the same bound volume. The final series of booklets were bound together within a slipcase and presented as a compendium of recorded events, further emphasizing the sense of a dossier of information.

Layers and Duality

Two different sizes of page were chosen for the final remediation. The largest page size retains the dimensions of the original novel: Crown Octavo (7½ x 5 inches), while the smaller pages are proportionally scaled to the same aspect ratio. Most of the time, one of the books sits within the other: the concept behind this is that Hyde is within Jekyll.

Some of the booklets are designed so that readers have two different ways of experiencing the story, either through the imagery contained in one of the parts or through the text contained in the other. In addition, although there are two different page sizes, in order to be visually consistent the text throughout the books is set at the same size and leading. The imagery used in the final collection comes from a variety of different sources but mainly from medical studies and examples from the very early days of photography, and in particular the work of Eadweard Muybridge.

Hernández attempted a range of visual approaches, including mapping the content of the narrative through simple notes, folding and colour coding (opposite top) and cutting through the text to reveal a further story behind (opposite bottom left). The final hybrid novel is grouped according to its underlying narrative tension into seven different booklets, containing the ten chapters from the original novel, all contained within one slipcase and presented as a collection of interrelated documents (next page).

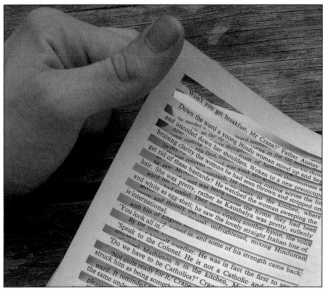

ve o'clock had scarce rung
...on, ere the knocker sound-
... on the door. I went myself
...ns, and found a small man
...inst the pillars of the por-

...e from Dr. Jekyll?' I asked.
...'yes' by a constrained ges-
...n I had bidden him enter,
...y me without a searching
...e into the darkness of the
...was a policeman not far
...with his bull's eye open;
...ht, I thought my visitor
...de greater haste.
...ulars struck me, I con-
...ly; and as I followed him
... light of the consulting-
...hand ready on my weap-
..., I had a chance of clear-
...had never set eyes on

11

him before, so much was certain. He
was small, as I have said; I was struck
besides with the shocking expression of
his face, with his remarkable combination of great muscular activity and great
apparent debility of constitution, and –
last but not least– with the odd, subjective disturbance caused by his neigh-
bourhood. This bore some resemblance
to incipient rigour, and was accompanied
by a marked sinking of the pulse. At the
time, I set it down to some idiosyncratic, personal distaste, and merely won-
dered at the acuteness of the symptoms;
but I have since had reason to believe the
cause to lie much deeper in the nature of
man, and to turn on some nobler hinge
than the principle of hatred.

This person (who had thus, from the
first moment of his entrance, struck in
me what I can only describe as a disgust-

14

Case Study 07: **Cypriot Identity**

As a Cypriot, Georgia Evagorou's initial intention with this type and language project was to respond to what she perceived as the failure of the Greek writing system to represent all the common speech sounds of the dialect used by Cypriot communities in informal spoken communication. Both spoken and written modes of communication in Cyprus vary greatly in relation to their use in formal and informal situations, and Evagorou's research question aimed to discover to what extent language is a factor in the construction of a country's identity. In order to provide an answer to a number of problems arising from her contextual research, she also decided to make a phonetically more adequate spelling system to reflect the Cypriot dialect. This was realized through the design of additional letters that aim to give Cypriots a better form of written script to express their language and their cultural identity more efficiently. The development of new glyphs was, then, something of a personal endeavour to reflect the complexity of the culture, and the social and personal politics of language in Cyprus.

Evagorou's primary research included a formal investigation into the range of language attitudes and modes in Cypriot culture. This involved a detailed survey of the usage of written forms (including Greek and Latin alphabets) and spoken dialects within a variety of formal and informal situations and contexts. A total of 1,038 Cypriot language speakers participated in this study, and the results were charted by age, location and the choice of writing system adopted by each user. Evagorou used this data within a series of information design charts to illustrate how people's speech patterns appear in different social networks, from personal communication between friends and family members to formal business reports, educational contexts and professional environments.

Diglossia

The term *diglossia* refers to a situation in which two dialects or languages are used by the same speech community. Standard Greek and Cypriot Greek are used concurrently by the same speakers within the Greek-Cypriot speech community, but under different circumstances.

Formal communication in Cyprus for both written and spoken communication uses the Standard Greek language and alphabet. Informal online communication uses *Greeklish*, a phonetic version of the Greek language written with the Latin alphabet. The spoken dialect is Cypriot Greek, though this varies in relation to the context of the spoken communication itself – formal situations use Standard Greek, while Cypriot Greek is more often used in social and informal contexts.

Evagorou asked whether the usage of Greeklish might reflect the fact that it offers Cypriots a better script to express speech sounds used in the Cypriot dialect than the Greek alphabet. Greeklish is characterized by spelling variations, whereby Greek characters are transliterated with more than one Latin equivalent. These transliterations can be of two different types – some are phonetic, attempting to represent Greek sounds/phonemes with Latin characters, whereas others are orthographic, attempting to maintain Greek orthographic conventions and representing Greek characters with visually equivalent Latin characters.

CYPRIOT GLYPHS KEY BOOK

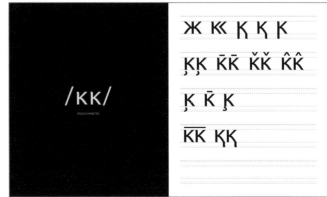

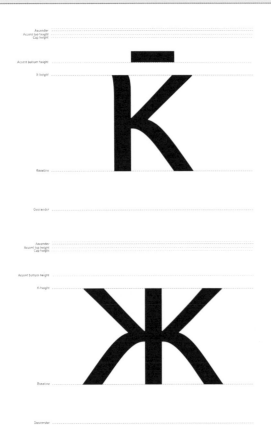

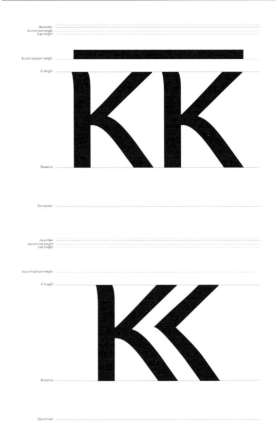

Letterform Evolution

Through her contextual studies covering secondary research on the subject of Cypriot dialect, writing systems and linguistics, Evagorou found that most studies ignore typography. She even interviewed a number of Cypriot linguistic professors who are working to create the first online Cypriot dictionary, and found that the possibility of collaborating with a typographer was never a consideration for them. From her own research path, she asserts that the explication of written language needs the expertise of both a typographer and a linguist in order to provide a complete description of its forms and structures together with a satisfactory explanation of its functions and effects.

As a Cypriot and as a professional graphic designer, Evagorou felt that creating new glyphs was more than playing with type, it was a fundamental attempt at proposing and testing solutions that could give an innovative script to Cypriots to reflect their spoken language more accurately. Variations in the development of individual glyphs were each tested with potential user groups, and she was careful to maintain a clear correspondence between the handwritten form and its evolution toward a typographic mark (above). These new glyphs were then refined and their proposed usage and phonetic interpretation demonstrated within more extended typographic compositions (opposite page).

κόαλον

ϗ

ΚΚ ΚΚ Ж ΚΚ ϗ

κόϗαλον

ΑΡΚΟΝΤΟΙ ΤΖΙΑΙ ΦΤΩΣΟΙ

Μες στο σιμηηρόχτιστον τζι ακάματον χωράφιν έμπηκα τζι είδα μνήματα, είδα σταυρούς στημένους τζιαί πάνω τους να φαίνεται, να μολοά, να γράφει χρονολοϊάν τζι όνομαν τους λάς τους πεθαμμένους. Τζι είδα τζιαί μνήμαν του φτωχού τζιαί του αρκόντου μνήμαν, με γύρου γύρου κάντζελλα, άγαλμαν τζιαι τζιβούριν, μά του φτωχού, του πάφτωχου, μεσάνυχτον πισσούριν. Τζι έκλαψα τζι ανεστέναξα τζι εχώστηκα στο κρίμαν τζι εφάνην μόσιεν η γη τζι ερούφησέν με κάτω τζι επήα τζι εποκούλιασα στα τάρταρα του Άδη. Τζι είδα μες τζείντην γερμινιάν, μες τζείνον το σκοτάδιν στοίβες, βουνάρκα τζιαι σωρούς κόκαλα των πλασμάτων. Τζι εστάθηκα τζι εθώρουν τα σσυφτός έναν καράριν τζι ούλα τζεί κάτω μνιά πίττα, ούλα μαλλιά κουβάριν. Τζι έν εξηδκιάλυσα τζι εγιώ κόκαλον μανιχόν του, να πω τούτος εν του φτωχού τζιαι τζείνος εν τα' αρκόντου!

ΑΡΚΟΝΤΟΙ ΤΖΙΑΙ ΦΤΩΣΟΙ

Μες στα σιμηηρόχτιστον τζι ακάματον χωράφιν έμπηκα τζι είδα μνήματα, είδα σταυρούς στημένους τζιαί πάνω τους να φαίνεται, να μολοά, να γράφει χρονολοϊάν τζι όνομαν τους λάς τους πεθαμμένους. Τζι είδα τζιαί μνήμαν του φτωχού τζιαί του αρκόντου μνήμαν, με γύρου γύρου κάντζελλα, άγαλμαν τζιαι τζιβούριν, μά του φτωχού, του πάφτωχου, μεσάνυχτον πισσούριν.

κόϰϰαλον κόϗϗαλον κόжαλον κόϰϰαλον κόϗαλον

κόϰϰαλον κόϗϗαλον κόжαλον κόϰϰαλον κόϗαλον

κόϰϰαλον κόϗϗαλον κόжαλον κόϰϰαλον κόϗαλον

κόϰϰαλον κόϗϗαλον κόжαλον κόϰϰαλον κόϗαλον

Case Study 07: Cypriot Identity

Writing Solutions

Evagorou's second research direction was to draw upon the range of potential contexts and situations identified within her primary research on the use of different language forms, with a view to designing a possible solution to a number of existing problems. She proposed that the incorporation of new glyphs within the spelling system might bring into effect a better and more appropriate use of the Greek alphabet when representing the Cypriot dialect.

She also recorded a number of negative attitudes toward the use of Greek Cypriot dialect, in particular in relation to perceived levels of educational status or 'higher' cultural value – such as in formal situations where Standard Greek is the accepted mode of communication. Some of these attitudes are possibly compounded by the fact that the Cypriot language is not standardized or codified in any way and does not possess a generally accepted orthographic system. Drawing on her studies into language and spelling reform, phonetics and the development of ligatures and combined characters, Evagorou set out to develop new glyphs to enhance the Greek alphabet with additional characters that can be used to express a number of characteristic Cypriot speech sounds.

The designer's criteria for these new glyphs included the need for them to be easy to learn, easy to remember, and easy to write. Any new typographic form has to have a handwritten basis: it is vital that letters are as simple as possible and easy to write. Readability and legibility of the new forms were also important factors that had to be taken into consideration, together with typographic styles and the ways in which the individual characters would operate within the wider written system.

Reformed Characters

Reformed alphabets often attempt to more accurately transcribe the sounds of a spoken language. Today, the most common system and one of the most successful accomplishments of alphabetic reform for transcribing the sounds of language is the International Phonetic Alphabet (IPA). Research into the IPA informed Evagorou's practical development, with careful consideration given to the evolution of individual letterforms, their proposed function and usage, and their typographic equivalent.

Evagorou's Cypriot letters were initially designed individually, one at a time. However, it must always be remembered that letters are rarely treated as individual elements. A single letter that works well may not harmonize in a word. Letters composed in a word behave differently from when they are seen in isolation. It was important to constantly review the letters in the context of other letters to test how they would work within a body of text (opposite page).

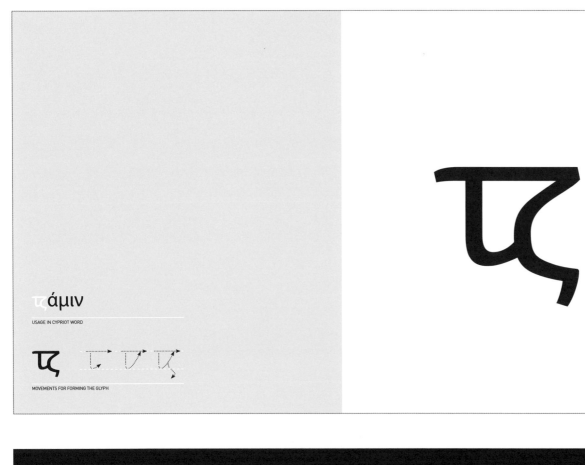

τζ τζ τζ ɉ

εφεντζιάστηκεν
εφεντζιάστηκεν
εφεντζιάστηκεν
εφεντζιάστηκεν

Ανεράδα

Αντάν με είδεν έφεξεν
τζι ο νους-μου εφεντζιάστηκεν
τζι εφάνην κόσμος φωτερός.
Αντάν μου χαμογέλασεν
παράδεισος επλάστηκεν
ομπρός-μου τζέμεινα ξερός.
Ευτύς το πας-μου έχασα
τον κόσμον ελησμόνησα
τζι έμεινα χάσκοντα βριχτός
είπεν-μου, έλα, κλούθα-μου
τζαι πο καρκιάς επόνησα
τζι ακλούθησά-της, ο χαντός
Λαόνια, κάμπους τζαι βουνά
αντάμα εκδιαβήκαμεν
γεμάτ' αθθούς τζι αγκαθθερά
η στράτα εν ετέλειωνεν
τζιαι δεν εποσταθήκαμεν
ήτουν για λλόσου-μας χαρά.
Έτρεμεν με τζαι χάσει-με
τζι έτρεμα μεν τζαι χάσω-την
τζαι μεν της πως, τζαι μεν μου πει
εδίφουν-την τζι εκαύκουμουν
τζι' έτρεμεν μεν τζιαι πκιάσω-την
τζιαι γίνουμεν τζι οι δκυο στραπή.

Ανεράδα

Αντάν με είδεν έφεξεν
τζι ο νους-μου εφεντζιάστηκεν
τζι εφάνη κόσμος φωτερός.
Αντάν μου χαμογέλασεν
παράδεισος επλάστηκεν
ομπρός-μου τζέμεινα ξερός.
Ευτύς το πας-μου έχασα
τον κόσμον ελησμόνησα
τζι έμεινα χάσκοντα βριχτός
είπεν-μου, έλα, κλούθα-μου
τζαι πο καρκιάς επόνησα
τζι ακλούθησά-της, ο χαντός
Λαόνια, κάμπους τζαι βουνά
αντάμα εκδιαβήκαμεν
γεμάτ' αθθούς τζι αγκαθθερά
η στράτα εν ετέλειωνεν
τζιαι δεν εποσταθήκαμεν
ήτουν για λλόσου-μας χαρά.
Έτρεμεν με τζαι χάσει-με
τζι έτρεμα μεν τζαι χάσω-την
τζαι μεν της πως, τζαι μεν μου πει
εδίφουν-την τζι εκαύκουμουν
τζι' έτρεμεν μεν τζιαι πκιάσω-την
τζιαι γίνουμεν τζι οι δκυο στραπή.

εφεντζιάστηκεν

εφεντζιάστηκεν

εφεντζιάστηκεν

εφεντζιάστηκεν

εφεντζιάστηκεν

εφεντζιάστηκεν

εφεντζιάστηκεν

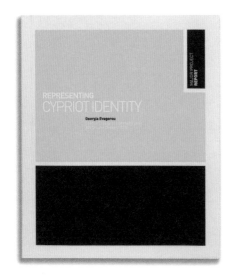

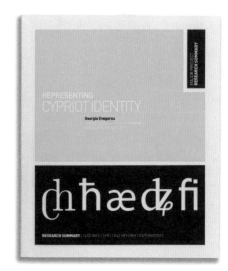

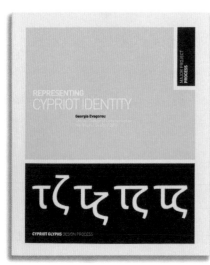

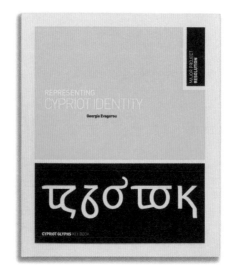

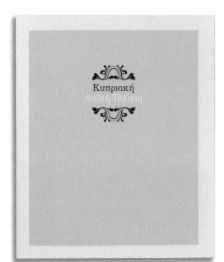

Final Books

Evagorou's research and development resulted in the design of one consonant and six consonant pairs of unique Cypriot glyphs designed to enhance the existing Greek alphabet when used by the Greek Cypriot community. The final resolution of the project took the form of a key book of the final Cypriot glyphs, together with a series of books outlining the evaluation of each research strand and the development of each letterform (above). The key book also includes the IPA symbols of each sound and the writing guide for each glyph.

In addition, she designed a book of Cypriot poetry demonstrating the use of Standard Greek forms within an extended text, set opposite the same poems incorporating the new characters (opposite page). Evagorou felt that this outcome could be read 'naturally' by Greek Cypriot readers, as the letterforms themselves were evolved from familiar forms, and the content of the extended text – the poems – were also highly evocative of the language and culture of Cyprus.

As the designer notes in her research summary: '…*as the values and identity of Cypriot dialect is inadequately represented when it is written with Greek characters, this book aims to acknowledge my initial target of providing Cypriots a better script to express their dialect more accurately.'*

Ανεράδα

Σε μιαν ποταμοδκιάβασην
μιαλ λυερήν εσσιάστηκα
νείεν καεί η σταλαμή!
ούλλα τ' αρνίν εις τον τσοκκόν
ο άχαρος επιάστηκα
αντάν πιαστεί μες στην νομήν.

Αντάν με είδεν έφεξεν
τζι ο νους-μου εφετζιάστηκεν
τζ' εφάνη κόσμος φωτερός.
Αντάν μου χαμογέλασεν
παράδεισος επλάστηκεν
ομπρός-μου τζι'έμεινα ξερός.

Ευτύς το πας-μου έχασα
τον κόσμον ελησμόνησα
τζι' έμεινα χάσκοντα βριχτός
είπεν-μου, έλα, κλούθα-μου
τζιαι πο καρκιάς επόνησα
τζι' ακλούθησά-της, ο χαντός.

Λαόνια, κάμπους τζιαι βουνά
αντάμα εκδιαβήκαμεν
γεμάτ' αθθούς τζι αγκαθθερά
η στράτα εν ετέλειωνεν
τζιαι δεν εποσταθήκαμεν
ήτουν για λλόου-μας χαρά.

Έτρεμεν με τζιαι χάσει-με
τζι έτρεμα μεν τζιαι χάσω-την
τζιαι μεν της πως, τζιαι μεν μου πει
εδίψουν-την τζι εκαύκουμουν
τζι' έτρεμεν μεν τζιαι πκιάσω-την
τζιαι γίνουμεν τζι οι δκυο στραπή.

Ανεράδα

Σε μιαν ποταμοδκιάβασην
μιαλ λυερήν εσάστηκα
νείεν καεί η σταλαμή!
ούλλα τ' αρνίν εις τον τσοκόν
ο άχαρος επιάστηκα
αντάν πιαστεί μες στην νομήν.

Αντάν με είδεν έφεξεν
τζι ο νους-μου εφενιζάστηκεν
τζι εφάνη κόσμος φωτερός.
Αντάν μου χαμογέλασεν
παράδεισος επλάστηκεν
ομπρός-μου τρέμεινα ξερός.

Ευτύς το πας-μου έχασα
τον κόσμον ελησμόνησα
τζι έμεινα χάσκοντα βριχτός
είπεν-μου, έλα, κλούθα-μου
τζαι πο καρκιάς επόνησα
τζι ακλούθησά-της, ο χαντός.

Λαόνια, κάμπους τζαι βουνά
αντάμα εκδιαβήκαμεν
γεμάτ' αθθούς τζι αγκαθθερά
η στράτα εν ετέλειωνεν
τζαι δεν εποσταθήκαμεν
ήτουν για λλόου-μας χαρά.

Έτρεμεν με τζαι χάσει-με
τζι έτρεμα μεν τζαι χάσω-την
τζαι μεν της πως, τζαι μεν μου πει
εδίψουν-την τζι εκαύκουμουν
τζι έτρεμεν μεν τζαι πκιάσω-την
τζαι γίνουμεν τζι οι δκυο στραπή.

Βασίλη Μιχαηλίδη

Καρτερούμεν μέραν νύχταν

Καρτερούμεν μέραν νύχταν να φυσήσει ένας αέρας
στουν τον τόπον πο'ν καμένος τζι' εν θωρεί ποτέ δροσιάν

Για να φέξει καρτερούμεν το φως τζήνης της μέρας
πο'ν να φέρει στον καθ' έναν τζιαι δροσιάν τζαι ποσπασιάν

Η ζωή μας εν για τζείνην τζαι ζωή μας τζείνη ένι
τζαι πως τρώμεν δίχα τζείνης τζι είμαστιν βασταεροί
εν γιατί με τ' όνομάν της είμαστιν ποσκολισμένοι
πον' το βκάλλουν που τον νουν μας μήτε χρόνια με τζαιροί
ξυπνητοί τζαι τζοιμισμένοι εν για τζείνην η καρτκιά μας
που διπλοφακκά για α ρτει τζαι να μείνει δα κοντά μας.

Τα λαμπρά μας ούλλον τζι άφτουν τζι οι καμοί μας εν σούσιν,
εν' συμπούρκισμαν φουρτούνας των τζυμάτων του γιαλού
ετσ' οι λας εν' που παθθαίνουν όντας ξένοι τζυβερνούσιν
έχουν μέσα τους φουρτούνας τζι αν τους έχουν προς καλού
τζι όσον τούτοι τζι αν καρδκιούνται που την Μάναν χωρισένοι
η αγάπη τους περίτου γίνεται δρακοντεμένη.

Πκοιος αντίκοψεν ποττέ του, τον αέρα για το τζύμμαν
τζι έκαμεν το για να αλλάξει φυσικόν τζαι να σταθεί;
Ομπροστά στον Πλάστην ούλλοι εν είμαστιν παρά φτύμμαν,
εν' αβόλετον ο νόμος ο δικός Του να χαθεί
τζαι για τούτον μιτσιοί μιάλοι για την Μάναν λαχταρούσιν
εν' η γέννα, εν' το γάλαν, εν' τα χνώτα που τραβούσιν.

Είντα γάλαν ήταν τότες τζείντο γάλαν που βυζάσαν
ας αμιλέψουν να το δούσιν, είμαστιν ούλλοι εμείς.
Αν περνούσιν μαύρα χρόνια σγοιαν τζαι τζείνα που περάσαν
'Πο μας ένας εντζέ βκαίνει που την στράταν της τιμής
Μητ' επλάστηκεν ποττέ του, τζι αν πλαστεί τζι ανοίξει στόμαν
νεκρόν εν να τον ξεράσει τζαι του τάφου του το χώμαν.

Καρτερούμεν μέραν νύχταν

Καρτερούμεν μέραν νύχταν να φυσήσει ένας αέρας
στουν τον τόπον πο'ν καμένος τζι εν θωρεί ποτέ δροσιάν

Για να φέξει καρτερούμεν το φως τζήνης της μέρας
πο'ν να φέρει στον καθ' έναν τζαι δροσιάν τζαι ποσπασιάν

Η ζωή μας εν για τζείνην τζαι ζωή μας τζείνη ένι
τζαι πως τρώμεν δίχα τζείνης τζι είμαστιν βασταεροί
εν γιατί με τ' όνομάν της είμαστιν ποσκολισμένοι
πον' το βκάλλουν που τον νουν μας μήτε χρόνια με τζαιροί
ξυπνητοί τζαι τζοιμισμένοι εν για τζείνη η καρτκιά μας
που διπλοφακκά για να ρτει τζαι να μείνει δα κοντά μας.

Τα λαμπρά μας ούλλον τζι άφτουν τζι οι καμοί μας εν σ́ούσιν,
εν' συμπούρκισμαν φουρτούνας των τζυμάτων του γιαλού
ετσ' οι λας εν' που παθθαίνουν όντας ξένοι τζυβερνούσιν
έχουν μέσα τους φουρτούναν τζι αν τους έχουν προς καλού
τζι όσον τούτοι τζι αν καρδκιούνται που την Μάναν χωρισένοι
η αγάπη τους περίτου γίνεται δρακοντεμένη.

Πκοιος αντίκοψεν ποττέ του, τον αέρα για το τζύμμαν
τζι έκαμεν το για να αλλάξει φυσικόν τζαι να σταθεί;
Ομπροστά στον Πλάστην ούλλον εν είμαστιν παρά φτύμμαν,
εν' αβόλετον ο νόμος ο δικός Του να χαθεί
τζαι για τούτον μιτσιοί μιάλοι για την Μάναν λαχταρούσιν
εν' η γέννα, εν' το γάλαν, εν' τα χνώτα που τραβούσιν.

Είντα γάλαν ήταν τότες τζείντο γάλαν που βυζάσαν
ας αμιλέψουν να το δούσιν, είμαστιν ούλλοι εμείς.
Αν περνούσιν μαύρα χρόνια σγοιαν τζαι τζείνα που περάσαν
'Πο μας ένας εντζέ βκαίνει που την στράταν της τιμής
Μητ' επλάστηκεν ποττέ του, τζι αν πλαστεί τζι ανοίξει στόμαν
νεκρόν εν να τον ξεράσει τζαι του τάφου του το χώμαν.

Δημήτρης Λιπέρτης

Key Concepts: Fitness Landscapes

Meme theory, or memetics, is a theory of cultural development that draws upon genetic models of biological evolution in order to explain the transfer and propagation of 'good ideas' within social or cultural groups.

Within this analogy, trends, beliefs, fashions and linguistic phrases are passed from generation to generation and through social groups amongst a process of imitation and behavioural replication, in a similar manner to models of biological evolution and genetic adaptation. Human cultures then evolve via 'contagious' communications in a manner similar to the evolutionary development of the gene pool of species over time.

The term 'memetics' was first coined by Richard Dawkins in his 1976 book *The Selfish Gene*, a hugely influential text on evolution from the perspective of the fundamental needs of genetic reproduction, which went some way to explain certain human and animal traits and characteristics as products of the genetic survival mechanism.

Memes, in Dawkins' terms, were theoretical replicators of cultural evolution, which acted in a similar manner to biological genetics and were intertwined in survival instincts among social groups and individuals within the same species. The theory has been further developed to explain technological, linguistic, cultural

and social evolution, the potential for artificial intelligence in computers, and even the spread of religious belief by other writers, notably Daniel Dennett and Aaron Lynch.

Fitness landscapes are used as conceptual models to demonstrate relative strengths and weaknesses in the gene pool. The concept of the 'survival of the fittest' design idea is actually better modelled as a landscape of peaks and troughs with the 'best' ideas higher up the slopes and those that will die at birth, or that are unlikely to survive, further down in the valleys.

This model shows that evolution is not about a single 'perfect' answer that resides on the peak of the mountain (where the 'perfect example' of the species might get struck by lightning or die some other unfortunate death), but a range of iterations that follow a contour around the higher reaches of the slopes. This indicates a good analogy for design as an iterative process, with the potential for a number of alternative paths to follow and potential solutions to a problem. There may be no single 'perfect' answer, but there are both better, and worse, solutions to the brief, and there is usually more than one way to guide the reader toward a preferred reading.

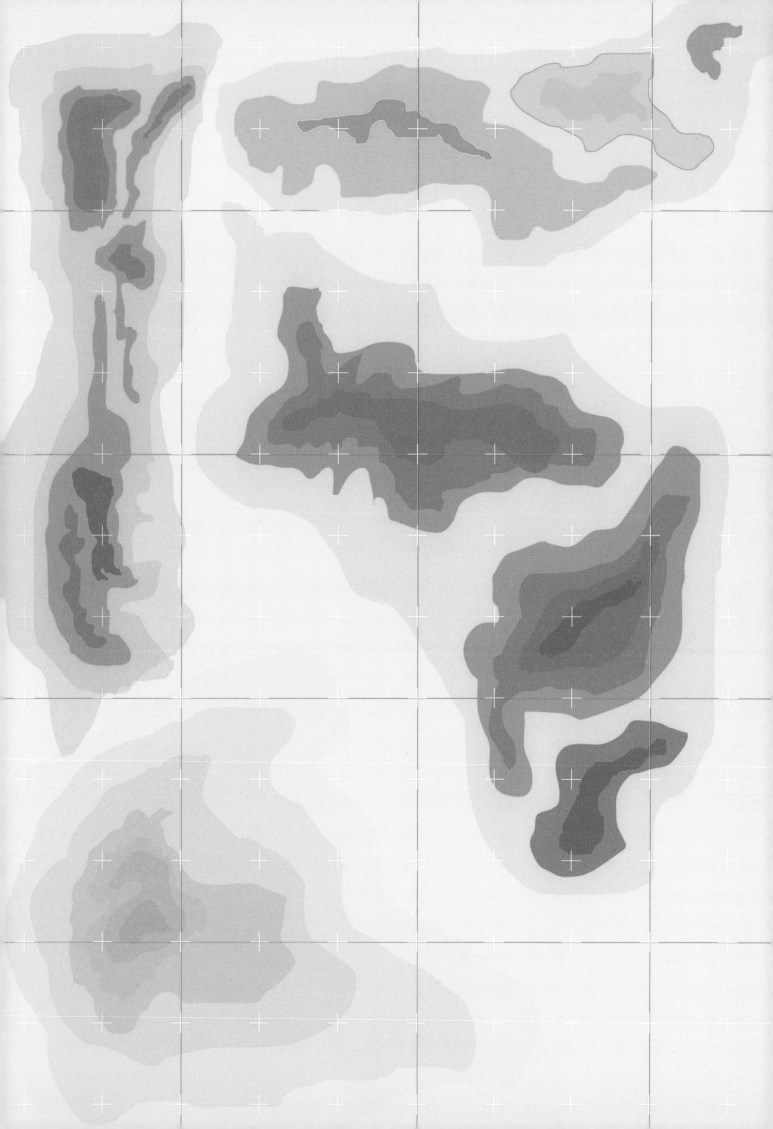

Exercises: Are You Receiving Me?

Objective

The intention of this project is to encourage you to explore the relationship between the word and the image and how when working in combination a wide range of communication ideas can be explored.

This project uses photography as its basis.

Part 1: Collecting Images

Working in groups of three you should produce or collect a number of images that address the following:
· Three images of yourself or yourselves as a group.
· Three images of objects that relate to you.
· Three images of the environment that you live in and that relates to you.

All images should be printed out at A4 size in full colour. Try to create images that are photographed in an objective or neutral documentary style.

These images form the foundations for Part 2.

Part 2: Building a Lexicon

You should now build a set of individual words that relate to yourself and the environment that you live in. These words should not be captions to the images you have created but should be words that have potential multiple meanings for the reader – they might relate to the meaning or context of the images but should not describe the images specifically. Try to build a lexicon of words without referring directly to the work done in Part 1 of the brief – it may be useful to select a theme to base this spoken or textual language upon.

Part 3: Word/Image Relationships

Begin to place the words and images together. Try to look at a wide range of variations and possibilities. The intention here is to find word/image relationships that

Key Texts

Barthes, R. (2009) *Mythologies*. London: Vintage Classics.

Baxandall, M. (1987) *Patterns of Intention: On the Historical Explanation of Pictures*. New Haven, CT: Yale University Press.

Buchanan, R. & Margolin, V. (1995) *Discovering Design: Explorations in Design Studies*. Chicago: University of Chicago Press.

Crow, D. (2010) *Visible Signs: An Introduction to Semiotics in the Visual Arts*, 2nd edition. Worthing: AVA Publishing SA.

Emmison, M. & Smith, P. (2000) *Researching the Visual: Introducing Qualitative Methods*. London: SAGE Publications.

Hawkes, T. (1977) *Structuralism and Semiotics*. London: Methuen.

Norman, D. A. (2002) *The Design of Everyday Things*. New York: Basic Books.

Pevsner, N. (1946) *Visual Pleasures From Everyday Things: An Attempt to Establish Criteria By Which the Aesthetic Qualities of Design Can Be Judged*. London: B. T. Batsford.

Poynor, R. (2003) *No More Rules: Graphic Design and Postmodernism*. London: Laurence King Publishing.

Rose, G. (2007) *Visual Methodologies: An Introduction to the Interpretation of Visual Material*. London: SAGE Publications.

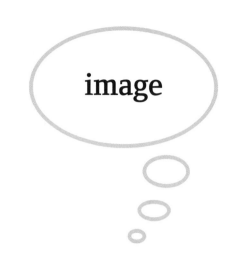

have possible multiple readings – words that unlock meaning in the images – not words that 'close down' the number of possible readings that each combination may produce.

Part 4: Word/Image Combinations

Once you have decided upon the most effective word/image combinations, consider how to place the type within or on the image so that both can be read without disturbing the effect of each other. Try to consider a typeface that is not too decorative and avoid fonts that may distract from the image. This font should be employed for each word on each of the images. You should try to find a common format and scale for each of the images so that a degree of consistency exists between them and that they can be read as part of a larger set or family.

Part 5: Arrangement

Once this is completed begin to arrange the image/word combinations in sequences that create possible narratives. Try to consider the multiple reading of each individual word/image combination as well as the overall readings the combined narrative may create.

This process asks you to consider how as a designer you can use image and word/type to create open and multiple readings for an audience. This should be undertaken with the widest possible audience in mind for the work. You should try to consider the scope of potential readings dependent on key factors such as background, age, education and culture. Each and all of these elements are essential considerations for the designer and should be a central part of your approach when thinking about how messages are communicated and, importantly, understood.

6. Process and Materials

Experimentation within the design studio: systematic approaches to the production of practical work and physical form

Practical Considerations

This chapter deals with the notion of systematic approaches and experimentation within the design studio through the production of practical work. Materials investigation is explored, within the professional arena, through the testing of appropriate form relative to a consistently applied set of criteria, and as a process in itself in the exploration of new and innovative visual languages appropriate to specific audiences or circumstances. This reflective process might be described as *'research into design'* – the exploration of design methods and practices, including visual testing and experimentation with materials and the potential of physical form.

Many creative disciplines within the visual arts arena place a great deal of emphasis on surface and materials – that which is termed the 'plasticity' of the image. In the field of fine arts, within areas such as painting and sculpture, for instance, the base materials (oil paints, acrylics, watercolours, pastels, bronze, stone and so on.) used in the construction of the work are crucial to the reading and understanding of that work. Similarly, photographs carry meaning through their material nature and also the context within which they are displayed: on a wall in a gallery or home, in a family album, within an archive. The physical interface between image and viewer is essential in the construction and interpretation of meaning.

One key difference with the disciplines of film and photography, however, lies within the nature of the image itself. The 'realism' of the photographic image, particularly through the use of colour film or moving image, can lead the viewer to read the content of the image – the scene depicted – but ignore its materiality (factors such as photographic paper, borders, mounts and frames, the physical presence of the screen or projected image).

Materiality
This relates to the physical properties of an object. In graphic design this might mean the physical nature of a book, for example, how it is printed, its binding, the materials it is constructed from and its status as an object beyond its content and functionality as a form of communication. An approach to design that focused on materiality would encompass the relationship of the physical properties of the book to its intended audience and the relevance of how it is presented as a whole.

This aspect of design is sometimes referred to as the plastic or 'plastique' of an object, in relation to the combination of a number of elements into a whole. With reference to the visual arts in general, the term is derived from the phrase 'plastic arts', in particular referring to three-dimensional art, such as sculpture. In the context of graphic design, materiality or plasticity can also refer to an activity where there is no physical object present – including screen-based, interactive and virtual environments such as the Internet or cyberspace.

As Elizabeth Edwards and Janice Hart indicate in their book, *Photographs Objects Histories* (2004), *'The prevailing tendency is that photographs are apprehended in one visual act, absorbing image and object together, yet privileging the former. Photographs thus become detached from their physical properties and consequently from the functional context of a materiality that is glossed merely as a neutral support for images.'* Where the material nature of the photograph does take primacy, it is usually within the field of the 'fine print' or in regard to conservation and the longevity of the physical support.

Art and Craft

Graphic design, particularly in the printed form, lies somewhere between artistic craft or mark-making and photographic realism. It lacks the supposed neutrality or transparency of the photographic image, but still usually foregrounds the 'internal' message – the content – rather than the surface material as the central conveyor of meaning. This is especially true in the form of the book, where traditionally a typographer would strive for clarity of reading *through* the typographic layout and grid structure. At the same time, the surface is usually clearly evident, as printed material or in the thickness and volume of a bound book, for instance. This materiality is often emphasized by the use of typographic elements and graphic symbols, which are read as a series of visual codes rather than a pictorial image. Graphic design is, therefore, a product with a complex range of signifiers – the visual lexicon of design vocabulary.

Graphic design… forms the connective tissue that holds so many ordinary visual experiences together. We don't usually view a professional photograph in isolation: we view it as part of a page, screen, billboard, or shop window display in relationship with other pictorial, typographic and structural elements determined in the design process. These frameworks and relationships are an indivisible part of the meaning.

Rick Poynor
'Out of the Studio: Graphic Design History and Visual Studies' in *Design Observer* (2011)

Tactility and Usability

Meaning is communicated through the plasticity of materials, the physical nature of the object (such as the weight and size of a book, or the thickness and surface texture of its pages), the printed surface and often the inclusion of photographic images, and the visual codes and languages of typographic detail and composition, colour, harmony, balance and tone. The tactile nature of designed objects that are intended to be held in the hand (such as books, magazines, packaging or postcards) carries meaning in a similar manner to the surface texture and brushwork of a painting, or the ergonomic nature of a piece of product design, though this element of the design is often overlooked in favour of the printed message and communication contained within.

The signifying nature of materials is important within certain areas of the graphic designer's craft, particularly in the communication of 'quality' or 'tactility' in fields such as book design or packaging, for instance. The graphic designer should therefore pay close attention to the materials with which their work is reproduced, particularly where the resulting object is designed to be touched or held in the hand.

At the same time, the denotative meaning of a piece of visual communication is usually contained within the visual forms arranged on its surface: a poster, for instance, which is designed to be viewed from a distance, relies more heavily on the visual composition of graphic elements than on the material upon which it is printed to convey its message. Viewed at close proximity, we may be able to observe the texture of the paper, the thickness of the inks, and the composition of colour overlays and dot patterns, but such forensic examination is not the standard function of a poster format, which is usually designed to be read from afar within a public arena.

Tactility
Perceptible to the sense of touch. Surfaces and objects can be described as tactile when they are designed to be felt, rather than purely seen or heard.

Tangibility
Capable of being touched or felt, having real material substance. This may also be extended to the outward perception or appearance of having tactility or substance.

Texture
The visual and especially tactile quality of a surface. Texture relates to the properties held and sensations caused by the external surface of objects arising from the sense of touch. Texture can also be used to describe a pattern that has been scaled down to the point where the individual elements that go on to make the pattern are not distinguishable.

10 Surface Texture >>
Product designers have long understood the value of physical materials and the sense of touch in the realization of designed objects. Graphic designers often operate within a similar field of operation, and the natural **affordance** of a surface texture – its tactile attributes – may be essential to the feeling being communicated.

Tactility and Usability

It should also be noted that the ephemeral nature of much graphic design output does go some way to explain the nature of designed artefacts as material objects. Necessity, budget and the speed of production can play a major role in limiting the range of materials selected to complete a project. The choice of paper for printing long runs of flyers or posters, for instance, is often driven by cost considerations, together with availability and the standard supply networks, account practices and technical processes of the printing bureau dealing with the production, rather than the tactility, quality or durability of the material itself.

Form Follows Technology

Developing technologies also play a major role in the material nature of graphic design artefacts. As print and screen technologies develop, so new working methods and aesthetic possibilities are opened up for the designer. The history of graphic design as a subject is inherently intertwined with that of developing print, mechanical and, more recently, electronic reproduction processes; from letterpress, lithographic and digital printing to the evolution of the world wide web and interactive digital technologies – with the latter now moving back toward at least a sense of a tactile experience through the development of sophisticated touch-screen interfaces.

Each new technology has seen a shift in contemporary graphic design aesthetics, and design historians have made detailed studies of the impact of each change in both working methods and materials. The development of increasingly sophisticated photolithographic printing techniques between the 1870s and 1950s, for instance, prefigured a widespread shift to the inclusion of photographs – rather than woodcuts, etchings and hand-drawn illustrations

Durability
The capacity to withstand wear and tear or decay. The quality of structures or forms of continuing to be useful or purposeful after an extended period of time and usage. The power of resisting agents or influences that tend to cause changes, decay, or dissolution. In relation to graphic design, these elements might include physical handling, heat, light or compression, for instance, and durability describes the manner in which the material surface withstands fading, tearing, distortion or corruption that might disrupt the reading of the design.

– within a range of inexpensive printed matter, such as posters and magazines. Similarly, the late 1980s and 1990s saw the development of a range of previously inconceivable design methods, which could be achieved only through the use of computer technology. The 21st century witnessed an explosion in the use of peer-to-peer and social networking through the Internet, together with the growth of multifunctional mobile devices for communication, information retrieval and social networking. Designers have had to adapt quickly to the potentials of these new environments.

The process of materials experimentation runs in parallel to the processes discussed in Chapter 4: Theory in Practice – but whereas the visual research methodology is primarily concerned with the composition and arrangement of visual elements, materials research follows similar investigations with the tactile form of the designed object. These two areas go hand in hand, of course: the materials always affect the surface aesthetic as well as adding to the complex chain of signifiers and visual grammar of the object, through which the reader or viewer derives meaning. Senses other than sight may also play a part, communicating through the size, weight, volume and 'feel' of the designed artefact. Through a range of tests related to the visual and tactile form of the graphic outcome of a project, the designer can help to focus the intended message more clearly in the eyes, and hands, of the reader.

It is necessary for designers to recognize the needs of the social and physical environment within which they work and to which they contribute, and to take conscious steps to define the future direction of their profession. For this to happen, designers will have to develop new tools, engage in interdisciplinary teams, initiate projects, and generate new information and share it.

Jorge Frascara

User-centred Graphic Design: Mass Communications and Social Change (1997)

Case Study 08: **Mary**

'Mary had a little lamb' was the first recorded sequence of words in the history of sound recording. As a homage to that legacy, Andrea Forgacs decided to call her proposed iPad music player application 'Mary'. This development was based on a project exploring the transition between a traditional physical music format – the long-playing record – and the screen interface. The result is an application that honours the 'old' model of the record sleeve and at the same time demonstrates a new way of listening to and enjoying music. Mary also draws a direct comparison between the tangible format and the screen, at a point in time where new, more sophisticated interfaces allow for a sense of 'virtual' tactility through touch and motion.

Mary is a simple and focused user interface. Forgacs felt that the incorporation of too many features would just confuse users, and would not benefit the purpose of making it tangible. Four key areas for development were identified: playing music, giving information, showing album art, and collecting albums. While the first two of these elements were to be developed through the proposed technology, the designer felt that the third and fourth, relating to the album identity and artwork and to collecting albums, should be a key feature that the application would build upon. As such, she decided that there would be no individual track listings or complex library systems, just 'stacks' of virtual albums with their original cover art and information.

In the era of digital distribution and storage, music graphics and information are a disappearing phenomenon. Albums usually come with low-resolution pictures and little or no information. At best, listeners are presented with a badly made PDF booklet or a small animation that says little or nothing about the artist, producer, publisher or label.

Reproducing Sound
In November 1877, the words *'Mary had a little lamb'* were the first ever recorded on a machine that could record sound and play it back. Even though it was not a very clear recording, Thomas Edison had developed the first playback device, called the Phonograph, an invention that was to change the very nature of entertainment over the following century, taking it beyond the limits of the 'live' experience and into the homes of countless listeners.

The phonograph was actually a by-product that Edison discovered when he tried to find a solution to a problem he was attempting to solve: the need to 'play back' recorded telegraph messages. The device recorded onto a tinfoil sheet by using an up and down motion from a stylus. Edison had inadvertently opened the door for reproducible music and speech. From the early 20th century on, recording and playing devices became more and more sophisticated, employing cylinders, discs and eventually computer hard drives to record, store and play back high-quality sound.

The biggest impact on music collecting and listening coincided with the shift to vinyl records in the late 1940s and early 1950s.

The dominance of this format lasted for some 30 years, until the advent of the portable cassette, compact disc and digital download. However, the graphic conventions of vinyl packaging still hold a powerful place in the hearts of music collectors, and vinyl sales are actually increasing again.

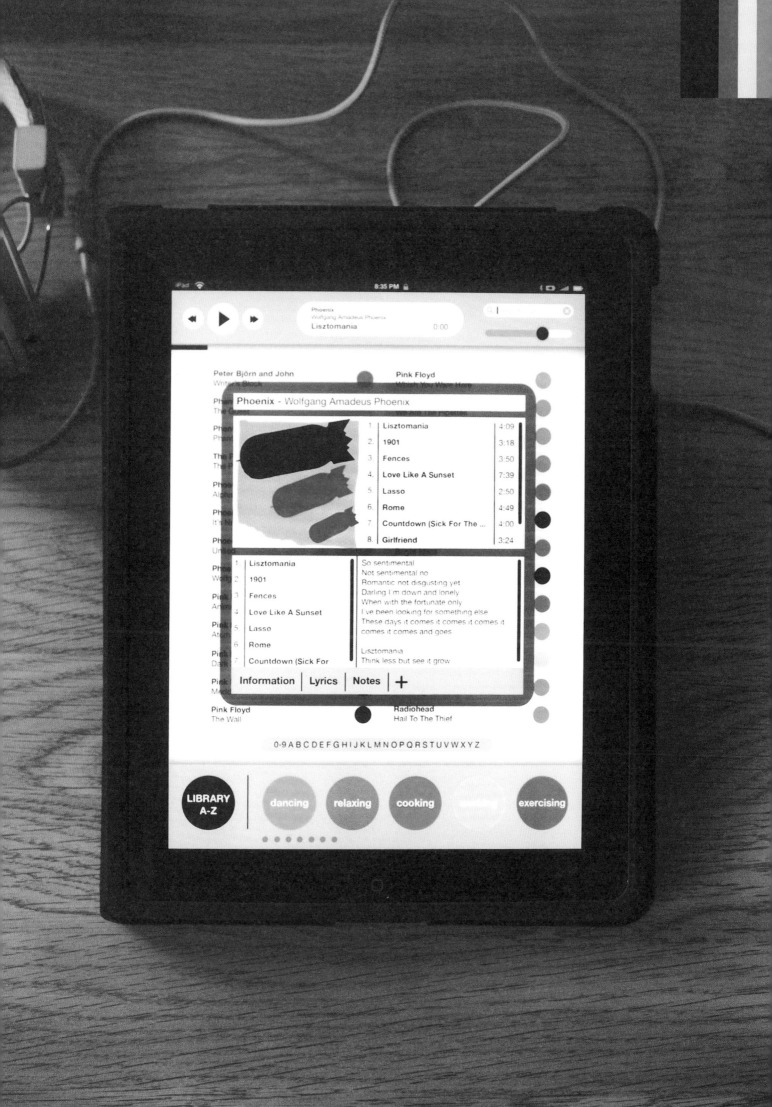

Case Study 08: Mary

To actually get to that information, fans often have to search the Internet or use complex applications to help them. This kind of information was traditionally a part of the packaging, a part of the illustration or graphic design, built around a whole interactive experience.

Now that music comes packed into zip files, some critics argue that the younger generation of music listeners have lost the ability to listen to music carefully in order to enjoy it. A study by Professor Adrian North, of Heriot-Watt University, concluded that '...*there is no more collecting music by album, there is only shoving as many single tracks onto the computer or MP3 player as possible. The difference to previous generations is that music in today's mass media is much more accessible and has therefore lost its selectivity. Music changed into merchandise — produced, shared and consumed.'* However, some music listeners seem to hold on to tangible formats,

and want to keep their relationship with the tangible experience of the physical album. Designers may see an opportunity to reflect aspects of the tangible object within the non-physical digital environment. Forgacs wanted to critique modern user interfaces that she felt did not value graphics and information, and ultimately to create a new interface that would give users a taste of the tangibility and collectability of the physical format.

The iPad is a new technology that allows users to interact with a computer using touch. Because of its size and weight, the iPad reminds us of actual material, such as notepads, clipboards or books. The user can flick, drag, drop, zoom in and out, turn the iPad, scroll, tab, pinch and rotate, all through the use of their fingers. As such, it triggers a strong connection to the object and is the perfect combination of the tangible format and the computer.

The Need for Information
Information was always an important element within 'traditional' forms of record cover art. It was part of the design and was usually included in every album release. Generally, this would include not just information about the background to the music and the artist, but also lyrics, liner notes and other data of interest to the listener: production credits, recording details such as location

and dates, additional musicians and other personnel and so on. The booklet or record sleeve provided the listener with everything the artist wanted their listeners to know about the album.

During the early stages of her research, Forgacs conducted a survey of a wide number of regular music listeners, asking them what information they felt they needed when selecting

or listening to an album, and their views on the positive and negative aspects of both physical and digital formats (opposite page top). She also reviewed the most common interfaces used by listeners, and gathered feedback on the relative merits of each. Once this information was collated and assembled, she was able to build simple charts to examine and highlight the ways in which users might benefit from a more visual

and tangible experience when engaging with digital music players (opposite page bottom).

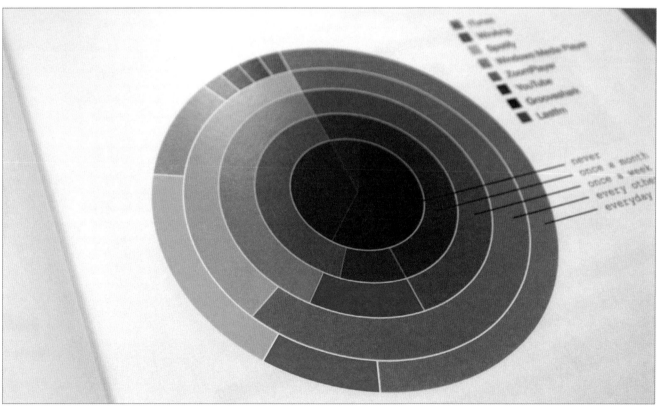

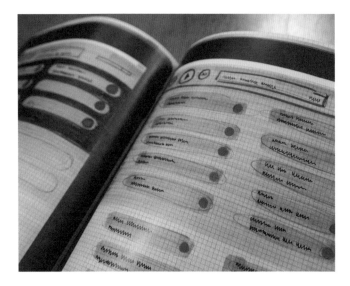

Mary Functionality

The final application is designed especially for the iPad, and includes a lot of the touch features that an iPad has to offer. The navigation is easy to use and clear to understand: Forgacs felt that the iPad uniquely suited the application because it allows all of these features to assist its purpose: to play music, give information, show graphics and organize libraries.

The design was initially worked up as a prototype model using notes and sequential drawings in the form of a storyboard (above left). Once defined, the interface was then developed digitally as a simple animation, demonstrating the sequence of choices open to the user (right and opposite page).

The visual style is very simple so that the functions of the player can be clearly understandable – iPad applications can't be as complex as a program on a computer: they need to be simple and intuitive without any unnecessary complexities. The use of big buttons and type was intended to maintain readability for all users, and a clear interface and simple menu

structure were utilized throughout. The colour palette is quite neutral and allows for customization by the user (opposite bottom).

The library interface is created in stacks (opposite top). The albums sit on top of each other and in consequence suggest the idea of CD or record stacks from the user's own collection. The library can be restacked to create smaller sub-libraries and groupings: for instance by genre, by favourite album, by importance, by room or by activity, thus enabling a feeling of involvement and control (above and right).

When an album is selected, the animation is made to appear as if the user is taking out a CD from a shelf: it pulls out and turns to reveal the content of the album. With a quick click on the title the album slides back into the right place in the library. When the cover art is opened it is possible to zoom in and out and to turn pages and flick through the booklet (right and opposite middle). This shows the user the cover in the best possible way on the iPad, and gives a sense of control and organization.

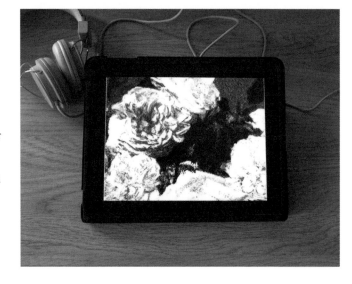

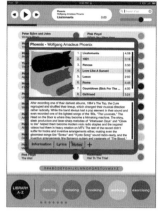

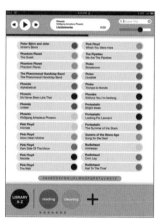

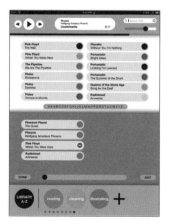

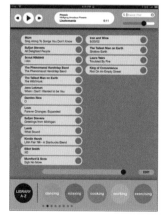

Case Study 09: **Message as Flux**

This playful and experimental graphic design research project is an exploration of contextual letterform: how typography can influence the context of creation and reception of the message, in turn emphasizing one possible understanding over another. Amandine Alessandra set out to conduct a series of practical experiments into the production of individual letterforms and textual messages, each addressing a given audience through the use of connotative clues. Based on her research into the space between visual and non-visual communication, she aimed to investigate the potential overlap between the right brain's faculty for synthesis and perception of concrete images, and the left brain's understanding of abstract words – between alphabetic and ideographic communication.

    The first phase of research examined how contextual letterform can be used as a medium to reinforce an obvious meaning or open it up to a new interpretation. Alessandra explored the creation of letterforms using actors and highly visible items of clothing. This concept of letterform created in the quick framework of a specific space and time while having to be highly visible led her exploration to what she terms *'the immediate form of message making'* within protest graphics. She was struck by a photograph taken in Nanterre, a campus near Paris, during the 1968 protests. The image shows Citroën workers and students wearing cardboard boxes, displaying one huge capital letter each. As they're holding hands they form the words 'Nanterre' and 'Citroën'; they become the message and have to stay together for it to exist, mirroring their fight against social class distinctions and cultural barriers. The contextual framework of the body, location and text then became a central aspect of the project's focus.

Letters in the Body
The flexibility of the casual form of typographic communication evidenced in the protest at Nanterre, combined with the performative potential of the group, drew the designer to start experimenting with forms of wearable typography.

Alessandra first worked on a series of three dayglo and black T-shirts, each with a slightly different pattern that displays different highly visible letters when seen from a distance, providing that the wearer places his arms and body in a specific way.

The three patterns were instigated by the three categories of shapes she found in the Latin alphabet: letters that could be drawn by shoulders and arms (A, B, C, D, E, G, I, J, K, O, R, S, Z), characters that needed more lines than the limbs could provide by themselves (F, H, M, T), and finally those that only required the shape of the arms (K, N, U, V, W, X, Y). When wearing these T-shirts, a group of people can form a word, a sentence or a statement. But what is really special about this mode of communication is that because a single person can mimic a whole set of letters, the message can change, from one movement to another.

This flexibility was slightly jeopardized by the fact that one single T-shirt couldn't be used to make every letter. Alessandra managed to overcome this issue by changing the wearable typography from a T-shirt to a bolero instead: a pair of dayglo sleeves attached together by a strip of fabric that could be worn across the front or the back of the wearer (opposite).

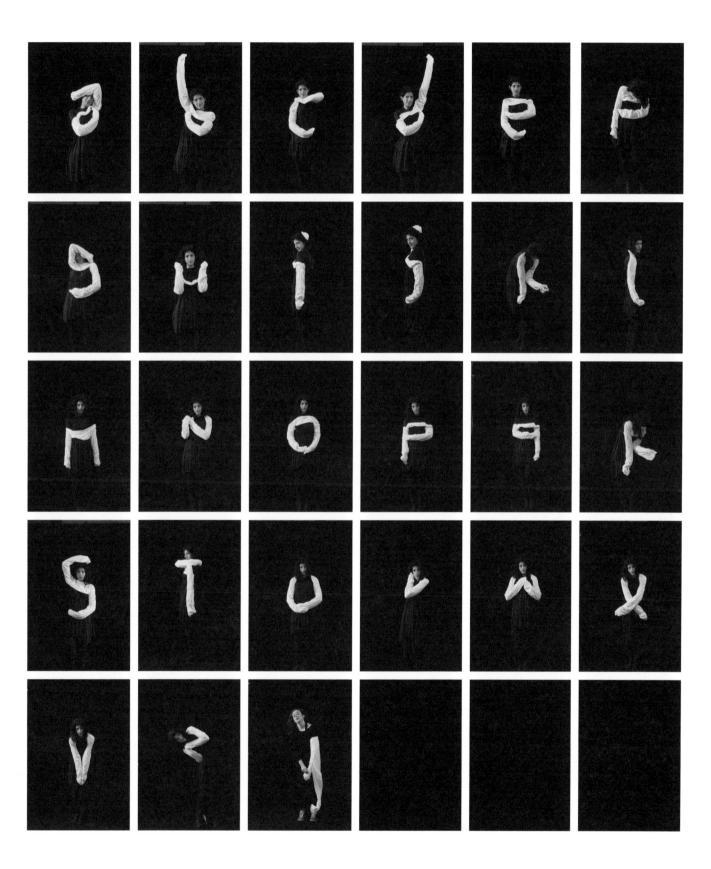

Reading Time

The superimposition of two kinds of information, one through words and the other through signs to be deciphered, became a central theme in Alessandra's research. She worked with a collection of quotations that were reinterpreted in site-specific constructions governed by one simple rule: they had to remain powerful once stripped of their author's name, where and when they had been written or where they had been taken from. Stripped from any form of context, these statements supplied the basis for early experiments aimed at using letterform for reinterpretation.

The experiment shown on this spread uses the concept of *relay* – instead of restating the content of the words used, the typeface gives it another dimension by changing its scale. The statement is taken from a quotation by writer Lewis Carroll: *'I have proved by actual trial that a letter that takes an hour to write takes only three minutes to read.'* The original context of the quote is the lost art of handwritten correspondence.

The sentence was reset by the designer in the mundane context of a rusty gate. The square chicken wire of the fencing was used as a matrix for the shape of the lettering. Because of the large scale of the typographic message (which now measured around 150 × 200cm or 59 x 79 inches) and the time-consuming technique of embroidery used, the statement literally takes on another dimension: it seems to refer to the making of the (somehow equally handwritten) typographic installation which took a long time to complete, compared to the much shorter time needed to read it.

Mapplethorpe

Another quote-based experiment was developed around a statement by Karl Marx: *'Philosophy is to the real world as masturbation is to sex.'* The phrase was set in a typeface made of shiny PVC-gloved hands drawing the shapes of letters in a rather sexually suggestive way, underlining the metaphor by illustrating it; the philosophical statement is made sexy. In this case, the process of *anchorage*

is not employed through merely juxtaposing type to an image, but by contextualizing the typeface with signs, thereby adding meaning to it, augmenting the signifier with features of the signified: the word gets closer to the thing it stands for.

Alessandra developed a full set of characters (above and opposite), giving the typeface the name Mapplethorpe, after New York artist and photographer Robert

Mapplethorpe, famous for his highly charged, sexualized black-and-white images, produced during the 1960s and 1970s.

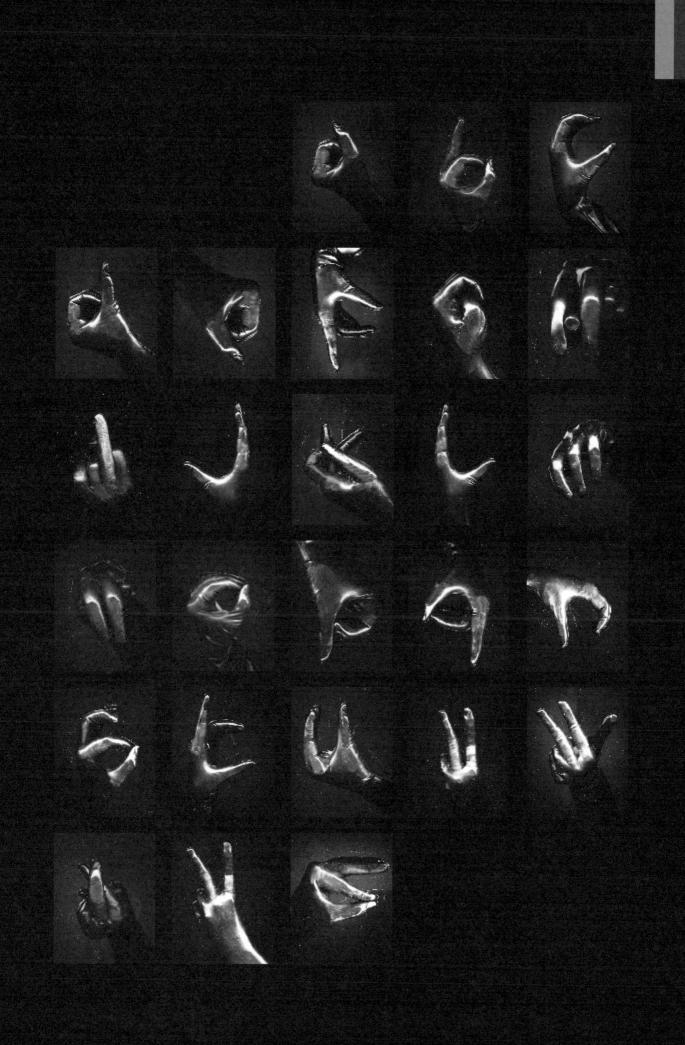

Case Study 09: Message as Flux

Extending Meaning

Word and image association relies on the faculties of both the right and left brain. If words can convey ideas while remaining in abstract spheres, images, when attached to them, tend to ground the message in a specific context. Although this pairing doesn't cut short all risk of ambiguity (sometimes even encouraging it), it can at least narrow the range of interpretations. Alessandra's first series of practical experiments engaged with both the construction of individual letterforms utilizing the human body as a contextual form together with site-specific narratives where the location and formal structure encouraged an alternative or extended reading of the text.

In *Mythologies* (1957), Roland Barthes explains how the juxtaposition of words and images can transform the initial message, either by reinforcing it (the image and text restating each other, a notion he

defined as *anchorage*) or by bringing a second reading to it by the juxtaposition of a word and an image that do not directly relate to each other. This latter process, called *relay*, is the one used by the painter René Magritte in his series *The Key of Dreams*. He depicted a grid of everyday objects with what seems to be a description written under the each of them: a closer look tells us that they do not quite match: a leather bag is captioned *'the sky'* and a swiss knife *'the bird'*. Despite their arbitrary disposition, we are led to seek a possible association between the word and the image.

Alessandra's exploration of the body, letter, location and message ultimately led on to the idea of typographic installations reflecting an abstract concept – time – and the exploration of possible typographic forms for the ephemeral message.

Action Time Vision

The final experiment of this research project took place in a busy train station during rush hour, chosen to reflect the pace of movement characteristic of the place. It involved eight people mimicking a digital clock in real time with their arms and shoulders. Standing in line side by side in the middle of the station, two of them acted as the hours units, two as the minutes, and another

two as the seconds. The two other performers were acting as the colons separating each unit of time. The wearable letterform, with its specific flexibility, allowed the message (in this case 'time') to change from one second to the other, following more or less accurately the ticking of the station's clock.

The numbers that each of the performers enacted were enhanced

by dayglo long-sleeved boleros, which besides making them visible, also echoed the yellow of the train schedule boards above them. Within this specific context, and using people as a medium, this temporary letterform confronts the economic value of time (as in the phrase *time is money*) with the individual perception of it.

The final outcome of this experiment is the recording of

the event, in the form of a set of photographs fixing the message in the time, space and audience (commuters in a rush) that it was addressed to (opposite page and next page).

Key Concepts: Affordance

The concept of **affordance** was first introduced by the perception theorist James J. Gibson in his book *The Ecological Approach to Visual Perception* published in 1979. The term has since been used in a variety of fields to describe human interaction with objects, including cognitive psychology, environmental psychology, industrial design, interaction design and artificial intelligence. Affordances are the range of possibilities that an object or environment offers (or appears to offer) to an individual (often termed an **actor**) in order to perform an action upon it. Gibson defined affordances as all 'action possibilities' latent in the environment relative to the specific actor or audience and their preconceptions of the form, materials and context of the situation. The affordance of an object or environment is then dependent not only on the physical capabilities of the actor, but also their goals, beliefs, and past experiences – often described as an individual or collective **world view**.

Donald A. Norman, in his 1988 book *The Design of Everyday Things*, extended the theory into the realm of product and interaction design. In product design, where one deals with real, physical objects, Norman asserts that there can be both real and perceived affordances, and the two need not be the same. More recently, Norman has further refined the concept to apply to the design of user interfaces and interaction design, noting that '…*in design, we care much more about what the user perceives than what is actually true. What the designer cares about is whether the user perceives that some action is possible.*'

The classic example of an affordance in terms of a simple everyday object is that of the door opener, whereby the presence of a flat metal plate would indicate that the user needs to push, whereas a grab handle would indicate the need to pull the door open. Norman goes on to explain how the reinforced glass panels erected on platforms by a railway company and used as the shelters for passengers were shattered by vandals, and subsequently broken again as soon as they were replaced, in an ongoing cycle of destruction. The situation changed when workmen substituted the glass panels temporarily with plywood boarding, prior to reinstalling new glass. Although the force needed to break the plywood was equivalent to, or even less than, that of the glass, the shattering stopped. Instead of smashing them, the vandals carved the wood or wrote on its surface. Glass allows us to see through it and can be shattered into a thousand pieces. In this 'psychology of materials' the affordances of wood make it rather more appealing to write on or carve than to smash.

TURN

PUSH

PULL

Exercises: Text Messages

Objective

This exercise asks you to consider the role of materials in communicating a message. Donald Norman writes that emotion and cognition work in tandem to create meaning and are both active factors in how we relate to objects. This understanding on the part of the designer can produce interesting solutions to projects based on a range of visceral responses to aspects of design, such as colour and materials, for example.

Part 1: Select and Analyse

Select a novel or fictional text and begin to break down the story into a number of narrative themes contained within the body of the writing. You should use both primary and secondary research methods to develop your analysis, referencing literary theory, historical and cultural contexts and reader interpretations, together with formal aspects such as grid structure, typographic styles and page layout.

It might be that the text contains themes underpinning the central narrative that may provide the designer a context to highlight in an alternative iteration of the book. Some stories deal with temporality – for example the novel *Dracula* by Bram Stoker – or it may be that the descriptive nature of the writing may permit a range of interpretations – such as the references to the sense of smell and aroma in the novel *Perfume* by Patrick Süskind.

Try to think about choosing from a wide range of texts – ones that offer a number of possible interpretations or readings. The two examples above are useful case studies because they have also existed in other media such as film and comic book, and these versions allow us to explore the process of how the printed word has been extended beyond the original authorial position of the writer.

Key Texts

Fawcett-Tang, R. (2005) *Experimental Formats v2: Books, Brochures, Catalogues.* Brighton: RotoVision.

Fawcett-Tang, R. (2004) *New Book Design.* London: Laurence King Publishing.

Frascara, J. (1997) *User-Centred Graphic Design.* London: Taylor & Francis.

Hochuli, J. & Kinross, R. (2003) *Designing Books, Practice and Theory.* London: Hyphen Press.

Johnson, B. S. (2007) *The Unfortunates.* New York: New Directions Publishing.

Mason, D. & Lewis, A. (2007) *Materials, Process, Print: Creative Solutions for Graphic Design.* London: Laurence King Publishing.

McCaffery, S. & Nichol, B. P. (2000) 'The Book as Machine', in *A Book of the Book.* New York: Granary.

McCloud, S. (1994) *Understanding Comics: The Invisible Art.* New York: HarperCollins Publishers.

Norman, D. A. (2005) *Emotional Design: Why We Love (or Hate) Everyday Things.* New York: Basic Books.

Perec, G. (2008) *Species of Spaces and Other Pieces.* London: Penguin Classics.

Rawle, G. (2006) *Woman's World: A Graphic Novel.* New York: Atlantic Books.

Safran Foer, J. (2011) *Tree of Codes.* London: Visual Editions.

Part 2: Alternative Readings

Start to explore how these other narratives can be revealed within the design of a version of the text. You should attempt to produce a series of iterations that successively build upon each other as you develop your ideas and their application.

When addressing projects of this nature, the establishment of the designer's 'rules of engagement' are a vital structure to work within. You might wish to set defined parameters related to the legibility or readability of the text – so that any successful solution may have to address how the text can still be 'read' and understood and that what is added through the design is an augmentation rather than a replacement.

This could involve the use of different paper stocks in order to establish a sense of mood or atmosphere.

Colour could be used to suggest the passing of time or particular time frames. Typography can be used to extend the meaning of the words or reveal hidden structures within the texts. Perhaps more importantly, a combination of approaches may produce challenging and unlikely outcomes.

A significant aspect of this exercise is the development of a range of alternative iterations that explore a particular aspect or approach; such as how to represent time in a visual manner. In this context it is better to focus on a smaller aspect of the text – one chapter, or an example section with strong references to the chosen subtext – and to build a range of design outcomes from there. The combination of design approaches employed can then be used to highlight alternative readings of the text.

Smith, K. A. (2003) *The Structure of the Visual Book*. New York: Keith A. Smith Books.

Sterne, L. (2010) *The Life and Opinions of Tristram Shandy, Gentleman*. London: Visual Editions.

7. Synthesis

The interrelationship between theoretical and practical models: applications and working strategies for the graphic designer within the studio environment

The Process of Synthesis

The concluding stages of any research project involve the convergence of the more successful and effective results of investigations already undertaken in response to the initial problem or idea. The models and methodologies developed at earlier stages can be assessed and built upon as the project develops through a process of iteration and moves towards some form of completion or conclusion.

In their everyday work, designers are continually involved in a process of synthesizing a complex series of factors ranging from technical production processes, budgets and deadlines to understanding the meanings of messages and addressing intended audiences.

Often the interrelationship of these factors will influence the outcome of a project beyond the designer's original intention. This is not to suggest that this process of synthesis is outside of their control –

indeed, a key skill as a designer resides in the ability to prioritize and respond to the various factors emerging in the course of a project.

Research inevitably requires the application of these same skills, but differs slightly in that many of the factors at work will be under the direct control of the designer. The parameters of a brief or research question are often established early on, usually during the investigation of the project's viability through the field of study and the project focus. As a suitable methodology is developed in response to this initial work, these parameters may expand or contract to encompass other aspects and that may in turn influence the methodological approach to the project.

The synthetic aspect of the research process not only builds upon the initial stages of the project but also offers the opportunity for critical reflection on the work in general. In projects where the designer

Criticality and Critical Being
The notion of critical thinking as a tradition within Western academic discourse has been developed by educational theorist Professor Ronald Barnett in his 1997 book *Higher Education: A Critical Business*. Barnett argues that a perceived limitation of critical thinking is inherent in its contextualization within the academic environment, rather than as a part of an approach to life in general.

Barnett describes an alternative notion of 'critical being', extended from the concept of critical thinking and defined as an approach to life that includes thinking, self-reflection and action: *'Critical persons are more than just critical thinkers. They are able critically to engage with the world and with themselves as well as with knowledge.'* In this sense, critical being is an approach to life, thinking and criticality that a university-educated person should

aspire to – taking their questioning and rational mind beyond the walls of the academy and out into the wider world.

has acted in an authorial or self-directed manner, its synthesis may also involve a reflection upon the less successful avenues taken in the work, as well as expected and unexpected results.

Visualizing Research as Subject

In projects where a particular theory or set of theoretical ideas have been explored and tested, the synthesis may require an analysis of how the initial work undertaken can be translated by the designer into a final set of visual outcomes. The questions posed by this kind of research may even result in a set of further questions or proposals as an outcome, encompassing a critical review of potential strategies and methodologies for further development. In this instance, the synthesis of the research may be in the exploration of the most appropriate visual form in which to present the work. This may, for instance,

result in work that establishes the context of the question(s) posed or may provide a commentary explaining how the questions were arrived at.

In applied projects, such as one commissioned by a client or a project rooted in a particular industrial context, the synthesis will entail the analysis of a number of detailed factors. These would include the historical and contemporary background to the project – taking existing precedents, established conventions, visual or stylistic tropes and the wider context of the work into account – its audience and its relationship to other existing work in the area under investigation, as well as an exploration of relevant media, including materials and production processes, projected costs and possible alternatives. This information will be combined with specific technological and budgetary considerations, and a reflection upon any testing and feedback that has taken place.

Intentionality

'Intentionality' is a useful term in graphic design in relation to the purpose or function of the designed object and the aims and objectives of its author or creator.

It is often discussed in philosophical terms, especially in relation to language – some philosophers argue that intentionality is characteristic of a concept or an intention. Within the field of philosophy, intentionality

is related to mental states, such as remembering, believing, knowing or experiencing, as well as to the concept of free will. In design research, a clear intention or set of intentions – such as *'I want to learn more about this particular design method'* or *'I want to solve this problem in a creative and innovative way'* – can help the designer to focus their project and to define a specific research question.

The Process of Synthesis

In commercial practice, a survey of potential strategies for development, alongside competitors and restrictions faced, would often take the form of a SWOT and PEST analysis – a common approach in the fields of marketing and advertising, which may in some cases have a similar relevance to design methodologies. This critique of the research question and the contextual framework provides the basis for the final stages of the research that will converge this information into an outcome or solution.

In some cases the methodology employed may be the outcome to the project in itself, rather than a developmental phase. This can take a number of forms including the documentation of individual but related tests, which chart the progress of the investigation. This is particularly relevant in areas such as materials testing, or in those projects that survey a subject area but do not attempt to reach a specific

designed outcome or resolution. Projects in this area would include Orlagh O'Brien's investigation into the mapping of emotions (pages 74–81), Becky Ford's survey of historical and contemporary memorials (pages 194–201), and Neil Mabbs' typologies of discarded artefacts passed on to charity shops (pages 114–123), all of which present designed summaries of the exploration undertaken, together with a critical reflection on the body of knowledge gained from that research, rather than attempting to define a particular problem or need.

As with any valid research question, the outcome of a project is not immediately predictable: indeed, if it were, there would be no need to undertake the research. It is therefore important to develop a degree of flexibility within a working research methodology. Often during the final stages of a research project, early ideas can be transformed

SWOT and PEST
Terms derived from market research and economics, SWOT and PEST are acronyms for two systems of analysis linked to the development of proposals or strategies and their predicted outcomes. SWOT analysis describes an examination of the *internal* Strengths, Weaknesses, and *external* Opportunities, and Threats affecting an organization or design proposal, and is used to make projections for the proposed research

activities. Typically the analysis seeks to answer two general questions: what is the current status of the proposed problem or question? and what is the intention or goal of the proposal?

PEST analysis describes a strategic review of the Political, Economic, Social, and Technological factors that may impact on the proposed project. It is a part of the *external* analysis when conducting a strategic

review or doing market research, and gives an overview of the different macroenvironmental factors that the designer has to take into consideration. It is a useful strategic tool for understanding the market and audience, business potential, cost and technological implications and direction for operations.

to suggest a number of unexpected or alternative outcomes. It could be argued that this flexibility is inherent in graphic design practice, and that it is part of the intuitive approach of many designers.

The Designer's Voice

Within the field of design authorship (see page 22), particularly research utilizing graphic design systems and methods in the interrogation of a subject of interest to the designer – research *through* design – the critical position or *voice* of the author is an important aspect for consideration. Relating closely to the designer's intentions, the design voice refers to the way in which the project is intended to be perceived by its audience: that voice could be critical, political, ironic, humorous, informative or educational, for instance. It may be transparent to a degree – in the typographic composition of a book or in many forms of information design – but it is never neutral. As a mediator and facilitator of communication, the designer occupies a unique position, and the axis between 'pure' translation of a client's brief and subjective intervention in the actual form and content of the message is at the heart of the debate concerning the social and political position of design as an engaged form of practice.

Creative Solutions

The methods outlined in this book are an attempt to move beyond the already overstated case for intuition and the designer's 'creativity' and 'imagination'. Often when the subject of creativity is introduced in design debate it masks a laziness on the part of its advocates – an unwillingness to engage in a more rigorous and exacting procedure for making, and a fear that, if revealed, it might alienate clients and audience alike.

There is a growing recognition that a wide-ranging education is needed for a synthetic and integrative field such as design to progress. By 'synthetic' I mean that design does not have a subject matter of its own – it exists in practice only in relation to the requirements of given projects. Design is integrative in that, by its lack of specific subject matter, it has the potential to connect many disciplines.

Gunnar Swanson
'Graphic Design Education as a Liberal Art' (1994)

The Process of Synthesis

Far from adding what has been described as 'intellectual glamour' to the practice of graphic design, the adherence and commitment to a method of working, grounded in research and practical methods with clear aims, is a significant development in the growth of the discipline.

In his essay 'Thinking the Visual: Essayistic Fragments on Communicative Action' (1994) the Dutch graphic designer and educator Jan van Toorn has described the designer as a *'practical intellectual… someone who is actively engaged in critical reflection about the designer's process of making.'* It is this activity of 'critical reflection' that van Toorn suggests is crucial to the designer's research. In fact van Toorn relates the notion of the 'practical intellectual' to an informed and engaged practice in general. This approach to graphic design is rooted both in the practice and a reflection upon that practice, and is

closer to the more accepted notion of graphic design (at least from within the discipline) as a problem-solving activity.

The American writer, designer and educator Andrew Blauvelt, in his essay 'Remaking Theory, Rethinking Practice' (1997), argues for a closer integration of theory and practice and a critical reflection in work, rather than about work: *'critical thinking and making skills are crucial for success…. Questions that cannot be answered with a simple yes or no are, in fact, research questions. And if the practice of graphic design is more than an unending series of solutions to never-ending problems, then we might begin to understand graphic design as a researchable activity, subject to both the limits of theory and the limitations of practice.'*

Informed Engagement
An informed or engaged practitioner in graphic design may well be operating from a distinct personal position with a number of central concerns in their work that extend beyond individual projects. Engaged practice may be driven by social, political, moral or other ideological positions about the function and consequences of design production. Debate about this area of working has informed the discourse

surrounding the discipline of graphic design in recent years and could be seen as part of the discussion surrounding the notion of graphic design and authorship (see page 22).

11 Cultural Signs >>
A text might be an image, object, artefact or place that can be *read*, allowing for historical, cultural or social interpretation. The El Morro National Monument is located on an ancient east–west trail in western New Mexico. Carvings were originally made at the site by the Anasazi Indians, and these were added to by further settlers from Spain and Mexico during the 17th and 18th centuries. As a

key watering hole in the western desert, the site became hugely important to US settlers heading west during the 19th century, and many left signatures, names and dates carved into the rock.

Case Study 10: **Memorial**

The Memorial research project began as a personal, critical investigation into 21st-century memorial design from a visual communication perspective. Becky Ford's initial research question centred on the need for a more meaningful and appropriate form of personal memorial in contemporary Western society, and the ways in which design approaches might be better utilized to respond to this need. A memorial is an object that will possibly remain in a public place for a very long period of time, yet today these pieces of visual communication often seem to be designed without much consideration; a pattern and code of practice developed in the past has become a set of formal rules to be adhered to without question.

We are also living in a time of increasing awareness of a range of human effects on our environment. Some people are quite literally taking this philosophy to the grave with them, through the incorporation of biodegradable and sustainable materials in both the burial or cremation service and the markers that surround these events. This changes the whole role of a memorial – it shifts from being a permanent, physical marker with a long lifespan to a short-lived mark that decomposes within a short time span. One potential arena for the development of such an impermanent or non-physical memorial is the Internet. Social networking spaces such as Facebook are already being used as a platform to memorialize the dead. As Ford explains, '…*what is remarkable about this is that people are doing it openly, sharing their feelings and talking about death.*'

In parallel to these shifts with the acceptance of a more open discussion of death, there has been an increase in the number and variety of vernacular memorials, often at the site of an accident or symbolic place associated with the individual's life.

Personal Marks

'A memorial is physical evidence that someone once had a physical existence here on Earth. The more eye-catching a memorial, the more loudly and publicly it proclaims it. A memorial can be a bunch of flowers, a headstone, an obelisk, a shrine, a tree, a cairn. It can be anything, just so long as it is something.'
Charles Cowling, *The Good Funeral Guide* (2010).

Through her contextual research, the designer found the vernacular road-side shrines and personal displays in cemeteries both touching and visually appealing, each telling us things about the individual being memorialized. Through these highly personalized spectacles, the viewer gets a real sense of who that person was, as the eclecticism of artefacts celebrates the life of the deceased in glorious technicolour and honest,

heartfelt messages. In contrast to this, official headstones and park benches are often devoid of character, impersonal in tone and sombre in colour.

Ford first mapped some common traditional modes of memorializing a departed individual, from a range of memorial stones to benches and trees. She screen-printed these typologies in a range of colours, from solemn black and silver to

bright yellow and pink, reflecting the contrasting range of traditional and contemporary approaches to the same subject (opposite page).

MEMORIAL

An object or structure established in memory of a person*

LAWN STONES

KERB DESIGNS

Front view   Side view

CREMATION DESIGNS

MEMORIAL BENCH

MEMORIAL TREE

*From the Oxford English Dictionary.

This list is far from extensive and is simply an insight into possible objects that are offered officially for you to attach significance to today.

Case Study 10: Memorial

These tributes challenge the more traditional markers of loss and remembrance. The vernacular memorial is becoming a ritualized norm, and its impact is being felt within more traditional environments: the memorials in our graveyards are also becoming more symbolic on a personal level and celebrating something of the life of the individual. However, many authorities are resisting this shift to a more personalized aesthetic of remembrance, taking the visual code of the cemetery back to what is seen as a more acceptable, sombre appearance through restrictive regulations on the nature of markers deemed acceptable.

Ford's research found that grieving openly at the loss of a loved one is recommended for psychological welfare: '...*we are beginning to do this as a nation but in an eclectic, haphazard, vernacular way. Some members of society may disapprove of these contemporary memorials, feeling they are littering our streets, creating an eyesore in public space. But if order is applied to these spontaneous actions then it may hamper their effectiveness in the grieving process.'*

The outcome of the research was not a designed solution to these issues, but a summary of the designer's findings. Ford decided that the most effective project outcome would be to design a series of books that documented all her research on the subject, as a catalyst for further discussion. The books lead the reader through a comparative analysis of the official and the vernacular. She argues that without religious rituals and frameworks in place, the form a personal memorial can take is completely subjective, and the most appropriate and meaningful forms of memorial today are those that celebrate the life of the individual. The very notion and uniqueness of 'individual' means that there can be no one solution.

The Order of Death

Over the last century religious beliefs have diversified in Western cultures, and many people no longer hold strong spiritual beliefs. For these individuals, the lack of ritual and understanding of their existence, coupled with an increasing disbelief in an afterlife, has shifted any common philosophy of the meaning of life, and with it an understanding of death, into a very grey area.

This has in turn affected how our wider cultures have visually communicated death-related matters and consequently has had an influence on the way we choose to memorialize our dead.

Notes and diagrams from the designer's sketchbooks and notebooks were included in the final series of books, displaying the research process and the ways in which her ideas were developing

(opposite top). Simple typographic comparisons of tribute messages on headstones and at vernacular memorial sites were also created as full-page spreads and a series of silk-screen printed posters (opposite bottom). Ford decided to communicate the contrasting messages in a simple manner, by reproducing the vernacular in luridly bright colours on a stock that portrayed the ephemerality of its character – newsprint. In

stark contrast to this, the official, permanent memorial texts were reproduced in very high contrast black and white on a heavy pure white paper stock that felt very permanent in comparison.

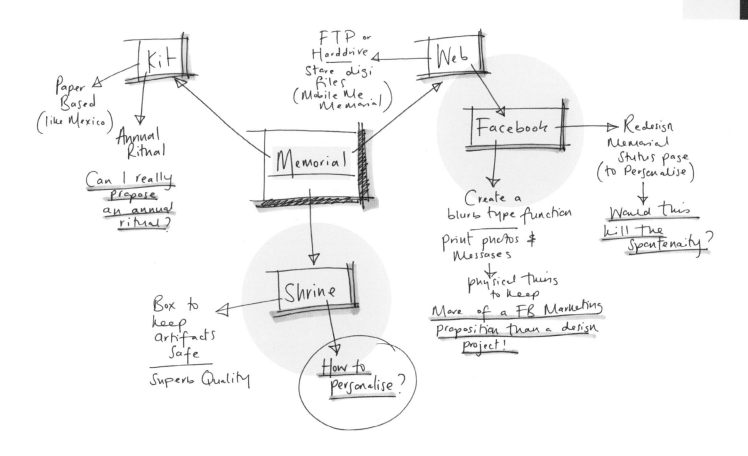

Kit

Paper Based (like Mexico)

Annual Ritual

Can I really propose an annual ritual?

FTP or Harddrive Store digi files (Mobile Me Memorial)

Web

Memorial

Facebook

Redesign Memorial status page (to Personalise)

Would this kill the Sponteneity?

Create a blurb type function

Print photos & Messages

physical things to keep

More of a FB Marketing proposition than a design project!

Shrine

Box to keep artifacts Safe

Superb Quality

How to Personalise?

GOD
GAVE HIM
TO US. HE
TOOK HIM
AWAY
TO
HIMSELF.

You may
not of known
this But you
was like an
uncle
to me.

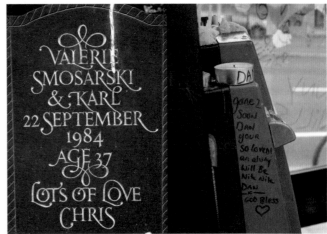

Death or Glory

Spontaneous, vernacular memorials have now become the norm for roadside accidents and murder victims in contemporary Western culture. This appears to be a turning point in the visual language of death for 21st century Western society, taking us away from the sombre and giving us bright colours and new secular symbols in the form of flowers, hearts, teddy bears and overtly personal messages.

The trend for vernacular displays has also extended to cemeteries, where plots are decorated with all manner of artefacts, ornaments and brightly coloured plastic flowers. These eclectic arrangements celebrate something of the life of the individual, in stark contrast to the monotones of the permanent, official headstones of the past.

Photographs of objects left at gravesides in cemeteries were

collected (opposite) and a series of typologies of personal memorials was assembled, both from traditional locations and modern vernacular shrines across London. These images were then collated into a book contrasting the 'old' with the new (above).

The use of full-bleed black-and-white photographs for 'traditional' memorials alongside full-colour images of more recent tributes

provides a direct comparison for the reader, and presents a strong rhetorical position.

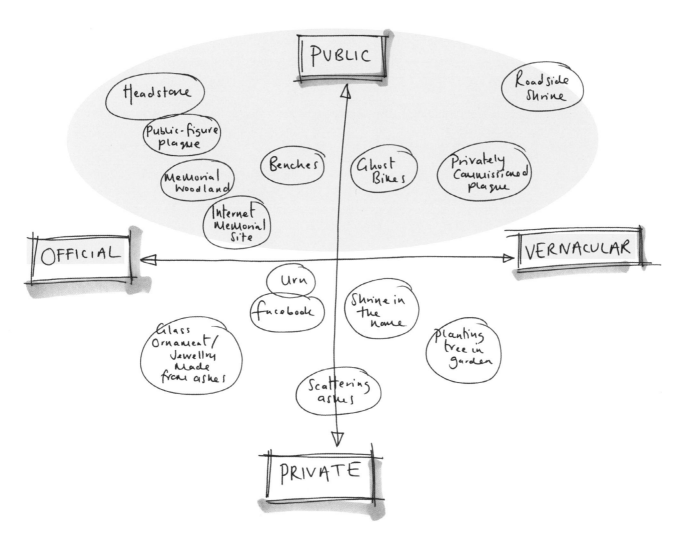

PUBLIC

Headstone

Public-figure plaque

Roadside Shrine

Memorial Woodland

Benches

Ghost Bikes

Privately Commissioned plaque

Internet Memorial Site

OFFICIAL

VERNACULAR

Urn

Facebook

Shrine in the home

Glass Ornament/ Jewellry Made from ashes

Planting tree in garden

Scattering ashes

PRIVATE

I love
you more than
words can say,
and I can't
believe
you've
been
taken
from me.

Remembrance Days

The public outpouring of grief following the death of Diana, Princess of Wales, in 1997 can be seen as a turning point in relation to British culture. Almost every theorist discussing the modern way of death in the UK today has cited this event as the significant point in the history of the nation in regard to modern death ritual. The floral shrines created in London and across the UK in remembrance of Diana formed the basis of many more low-key vernacular memorials that were to follow.

One of the issues surrounding death for those with secular beliefs is the lack of acknowledgement for its existence – there is a tendency to sweep it under the carpet and only deal with it when it is unavoidable. However, psychologists believe that modern communities need to address the problem more directly in order to cope with it better, and Ford's aim was to create a platform that could open up this discourse in a way that is not too dark or depressing.

Design experiments conducted during the research included the production of posters employing colour and tone contrasts for traditional and contemporary images of memorials (above), together with a series of images documenting the decay of floral tributes over time (opposite).

Case Study 11: **Happiness – todayifeel**

This project, entitled *todayifeel*, uses design to investigate the idea of happiness. Through a series of visual experiments, using projections in public spaces as a core working method, Kenzo Kramarz explored three levels of happiness as defined by behavioural scientists – joy and pleasure; well-being and satisfaction; and success and fulfilment.

Despite its evident relevance and increasing interest to the general public, graphic design has not been used specifically to investigate, interrogate, and explore the concept of happiness. That is not to say that graphic design is not utilized in the promotion and communication of a wide range of themes related to the subject – brands constantly strive to represent happiness by referring to the attainment of pleasurable experiences in their advertisements (once the consumer has bought the product, of course). The design industry has indiscriminately used conventions of happiness to create what branding gurus call 'a strong emotional connection between a target market and a brand'. Kramarz decided to take a different approach to the subject: rather than spending time creating this superficial layer of information, he decided to instead focus on developing the idea of generating true experiences of joy, which would aim to improve people's satisfaction without being attached to a product, sales or marketing strategy.

In general terms, happiness suggests things turning out to be better than expected. In order to theorise what he terms the *'semantic terrain of happiness'*, Daniel Nettle of the Centre for Behaviour & Evolution at Newcastle University defined three different senses of happiness. The first, termed Level One by Nettle, is the most immediate and direct sense of happiness and involves short-term momentary feelings of joy and pleasure.

Are You Happy Now?

It is possible to regard visual communication as an act or a process rather than a thing, an artefact or product. In this context design can be seen as an action intended to create a response or modify an attitude for example. The project created by Kramarz is situated in an emerging debate amongst designers about a more emotional and social form of engagement. The Austrian designer Stefan Sagmeister has described this in his own work by asking the question *'…can design touch someone's heart?'*

If very distinct social groups share the same notion about basic human feelings, what can be said specifically about happiness? Most researchers seem to agree that the notion of happiness might differ considerably from one culture to another. However, most of them draw a distinction between a more immediate sense of happiness (such as joy) and something more lasting (such as satisfaction). Kramarz carried out a series of practical experiments in order to test different languages, graphic approaches, media and, subsequently, visual resolutions that respond directly to each of the three levels of happiness defined by Daniel Nettle.

The work encompassed a range of print-based experiments along with large-scale public interventions utilizing motion graphics and digital projection. These experiments were intended to involve participants in site-specific responses to each level of happiness, from the unexpected pleasant surprise at Level One to the more critically reflective consideration of personal achievement and satisfaction at Level Two and Level Three.

Evening Standard
HAPPINESS THIS WAY
London Evening Standard
TOMORROW'S NEWS TODAY

Case Study 11: Happiness – todayifeel

These feelings are brought about by a desired state being attained, very often unexpectedly. It is most often created in situations involving more emotional and transient circumstances on the part of the viewer or actor, and may be viewed in relation to a pleasant, unexpected surprise.

Level Two is the one more often studied by researchers. In simple terms, a sense of 'satisfaction' might be defined as the result of the balance one makes upon reflection of both positive and negative aspects of life. It can be described as a hybrid between emotion and the judgment of emotion. Happiness is then a sense of well-being on the part of the actor, as a result of seeing the good aspects of his or her life as outweighing the bad.

Level Three refers to the aspects of life in which the person fulfils their true potential. This level can also be described as the attainment of whatever

a person wants. It is much more complex to measure as it also includes other variables beyond Level Two happiness, such as personal growth, self-directedness and relationship to the environment. It has a deeper sense of morality and politics – and is also affected by consumerism. Advertising and marketing strategies seek to instil a sense of desire for the products that they promote, and Level Three happiness may either reflect these aspirations or reject them.

The *todayifeel* project questions how design can be used as a tool that enables us to view our understanding of happiness in a wider context: the sense of personal well-being, life goals, objectives and purposes in relation to society and the environment, rather than the accumulation of wealth, products and the achievement of status or admiration.

Everybody's Happy Nowadays
The core idea of this project was the investigation, through graphic design, of the three defined levels of happiness. After narrowing down the focus and the context, Kramarz attempted to translate Nettle's psychological definitions of the semantic terrain of happiness into a framework that could enable him to interpret the subject from a designer's perspective. The intention was to underline the broader conceptual intersection between the three levels of happiness as well as to identify the specific characteristics of each of them individually. On the one hand, they are part of the same research area, but on the other each level has a very distinct personality – and the challenge here was to build up a framework to clearly identify the differences and how they could be expressed in visual terms.

The framework for the design interventions was defined and adjusted following a series of preliminary graphic experiments to determine keywords and voice, mood board and colour information, message and audience, experience, and possible locations associated with each level of happiness (opposite page top).

The designer's intention was to confirm the potential of graphic design to raise awareness and to mobilize society towards worthwhile causes, as well as to reflect the sense of happiness for participants at each location. Simple graphic diagrams were also developed by Kramarz as a personal critique of the ways in which advertising promotes a sense of happiness through consumerism (opposite page bottom).

LEVEL 1

 LEVEL 2

 LEVEL 3

Momentary feelings
JOY
PLEASURE

Judgment about feelings
WELL-BEING
SATISFACTION

Quality of life
FLOURISHING
FULFILLING

MOOD BOARD – COLOUR

EXPERIENCE – AUDIENCE

More individual, absolute experience.

More personal, reflective experience.

More collective (society-related issues) experience.

POSSIBLE LOCATIONS

Public squares, parks, or touristic sites. Residential areas in general. Locations where people usually feel bad, stressed, etc. To enhance the tension: industrial sites, unattractive or dodgy areas, abandoned places.

'Impersonal' locations, such as industrial sites or old factories. Public squares, university buildings (concentration of young people). Areas with no 'permission' for self-expression.

Well-established institutions, like financial or educational buildings. Existing billboards, commercial areas (such as Oxford Street or Piccadilly Circus). Locations that represent a specific social issue.

←

→

MORE IMMEDIATE
MORE SENSUAL AND EMOTIONAL
MORE RELIABLY MEASURABLE
MORE ABSOLUTE

MORE COGNITIVE
MORE RELATIVE
MORE MORAL AND POLITICAL
CULTURAL NORMS AND VALUES

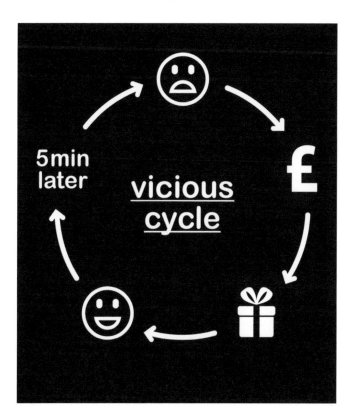

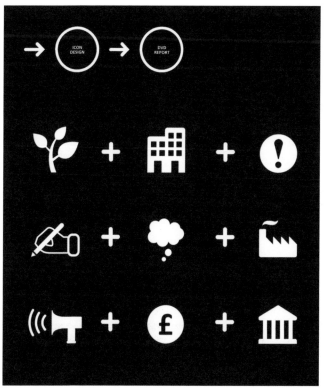

Unknown Pleasures

During his research into the nature of visual representations of joy and pleasure, Kramarz analysed a range of stock image websites and photographic blogs. He found that images of nature are habitually associated with joy, pleasure and relaxation in a wide range of distinct cultures. He also set up a questionnaire to ask respondents what kinds of images they associated with joyful feelings.

Visual representations of nature or natural events (blue sky, beaches, trees, ocean waves, snow, and so on) were the most popular result.

For his first public intervention, Kramarz chose to explore the notion of an unexpected visual event, drawing on images of nature that might be associated with the first level of happiness. The intention was to bring a visual representation of nature to a densely urbanized location in central London. Although green areas such as parks are part of everyday life for Londoners, the ocean and sea life are certainly not. The idea therefore was to transform a building into an imaginary, improbable fish tank.

Kramarz constructed a looped and overlaid video of a fish swimming, creating a shoal of white fish – the colour chosen to enhance the light contrast. He then projected the video onto a building in central London, with visually striking results (above and opposite page). Passers-by in the street were not indifferent to the shoal of giant fish moving smoothly on the concrete, and became engaged in conversations as to the nature and intention of the film, while at the same time smiling and responding positively to this unexpected and pleasant surprise.

Image 17 | Fish experiment / projection in Shouldham Street, London W1

Image 18 | Chalk experiment / projection in Crawford Place, London W1.

I Just Can't Be Happy Today

Level Two happiness was slightly more complex: Kramarz set out to create an experience that encouraged participants to engage in a process of self-reflection regarding recent life events or a personal judgment about feelings.

As a starting point, he decided that turning such an individual and introspective ritual into a collective and therefore shared experience could be an engaging way to address the question. The designer asked a group of people to make a brief reflection on the subject of happiness, writing with chalk on a blackboard. Calligraphy, rhythm, texture, and timing of people's writings were all very relevant information to complement the content. He constructed a very simple set to record footage of these writings, and then chose a location for the projection with a deliberately inhospitable, cold, and impersonal look and feel. The intention was to enhance the experience, boosting the tension between content and location (above right).

The relation between money and happiness has always been contentious. Kramarz wanted to create an experiment that could be a reflection about the uncertainties of the subject. He also wanted to match location and content, and chose a local branch of a bank for his final intervention. Quotes about money in relation to happiness were previously gathered in the research survey, and arguments about this controversial correlation were divided into two groups: in favour (blue) and against (white). They were both presented in a moving, pixel typeface mimicking the format of financial data in stock exchange panels (opposite page).

Image 19 | Bank experiment / projection in Edgware Road, London W2

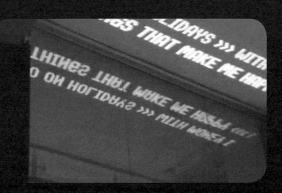

NEY MAKES ME HAPPY BECAUSE I

MONEY HAS NOTHING TO DO WITH

SHOES! >>> MONEY MAKES ME HAP

MONEY CAN'T BUY EVERYTHING <

CAUSE I CAN BUY LOTS OF SHOES!

S <<< I DON'T REALLY CARE ABOUT

AVING A BEER >>> MONEY MAKES M

Y IS ANOTHER KIND OF BURDEN <<<

Key Concepts: Modernism and Postmodernism

Modernism is a term that describes the range of art, design and architectural movements and subsequent ideas that emerged during the first half of the 20th century, also referred to as the modern movement. In reaction to the craft movement and ideas surrounding decoration and adornment, practitioners developed a new approach that celebrated the possibilities of new technologies and methods of mass production in order to enable a better society for all.

Many of the art and design movements connected to modernism, such as **De Stijl**, **constructivism** and the **Bauhaus movement**, endeavoured to celebrate functionalism and rationality under the guiding maxim that 'form follows function'. The modernist approach to graphic design focused upon the use of white space and sans serif typography that utilized asymmetry. This was driven by an adherence to the grid, based on geometry and the proportion of the page, as a controlling device.

Postmodernism is a movement that grew out of a rejection of the ideas of modernism toward the end of the 20th century. Significantly many of the original values of modernism had, by the late 1960s, become regarded by designers as dogmatic and only offering a fixed view or superficial style. Some designers also felt that the original ideology of social progression and universal benefit that could be derived from modernist design had to an extent been corrupted by the adoption of Swiss modernism in graphic design as the sophisticated visual language of corporate business.

Postmodernism celebrated a return to earlier ideas of the value of decoration and stylistic image-making. Rejecting order or discipline in favour of expression and intuition, many of the key progenitors within the field emanated originally from schools, such as Basel in Switzerland and later the Cranbrook Academy of Art in the US, and were tutored by central figures such as Wolfgang Weingart and Katherine and Michael McCoy.

The postmodern lexicon of historical reference, decoration, wit and the ironic employment of vernacular or non-designed elements, such as hand-drawn typography, constitutes a departure from the rationality of earlier approaches. This significant development brought about a reappraisal of the process of visual communication with design. Embracing ideas from architecture and 20th-century philosophy and semiotics, practitioners have attempted to advance the discussion of how relevant approaches, related to specific groups or cultures, could be developed, rather than aspiring to a universal language.

Exercises: Practical Methods

Objective

The aim of this exercise is to enable you to construct a self-initiated project. Often designers look to develop work outside of the 'day job' – exploring ideas about design and their own practice that do not necessarily fit within specific commercial briefs and that provide opportunities to investigate a wider range of ideas that will contribute to their ongoing development as designers. Many design courses include a degree of self-initiated work and often this is a focus for final examination.

When considering how to construct a self-initiated brief you should begin by thinking about personal areas of interest: things you are excited about or concerns you may have, for example – in short, issues you are passionate about. However, the project should be related to graphic design in either its subject or working methodology (or both). Initial thinking about project topics should reflect your knowledge, critical position and interests, and should be seen as opportunities to make use of the expertise, understanding, and skills you have acquired to date.

The following questions will allow you to structure your project and should be considered as the foundations of a successful approach:

Why?

Has the research question been stated?
Have project objectives been defined in relation to your broad intentions?

What?

What specific questions will the project seek to ask?
Is the focus of the project clearly described?
Has the context of the project been clearly described?

Key Texts

Barnett, R. (1997) *Higher Education: A Critical Business*. London: Open University Press.

Barthes, R. (1993) *Image – Music – Text*. London: Fontana Books.

Baxandall, M. (1987) *Patterns of Intention: On the Historical Explanation of Pictures*. New Haven, CT: Yale University Press.

Berger, J. (2008) *Ways of Seeing*. London: Penguin Classics.

Crow, D. (2010) *Visible Signs: An Introduction to Semiotics*, 2nd edition. Worthing: AVA Publishing SA.

Emmison, M. & Smith, P. (2000) *Researching the Visual: Introducing Qualitative Methods*. London: SAGE Publications.

Frascara, J. (1997) *User-Centred Graphic Design*. London: Taylor & Francis.

Harvey, C. (1995) *Databases in Historical Research: Theory, Methods and Applications*. London: Palgrave Macmillan.

Laurel, B. (ed.) (2004) *Design Research: Methods and Perceptions*. Cambridge, MA: MIT Press.

Lupton, L. & Abbott Miller, J. (1999) *Design, Writing, Research: Writing on Graphic Design*. London: Phaidon.

Norman, D. A. (2002) *The Design of Everyday Things*. New York: Basic Books.

O'Sullivan, T., Hartley, J., Saunders, D., Montgomery, M. & Fiske, J. (1994) *Key Concepts in Communication and Cultural Studies*. London: Routledge.

How?

Is the methodology clear and understandable?
Is the project adequately defined in terms of its primary research? (e.g. data gathering, formulation of design concepts and messages, critical reflection and evaluation, consideration of audience, selection of appropriate media/formats, articulation of visual language, media testing).
Is the project adequately defined in terms of its secondary research? (e.g. an interrogation of the field of study, analysis of reference materials, examination of alternative approaches and existing work within the field, relation to wider cultural contexts).

Who?

Has a potential audience been identified?
Is audience significant to the project and in what way?

When?

Does the methodology identify clear stages of development?
Has a detailed work-plan/ timetable been prepared?

Where?

Are the general research reference materials relevant, detailed, accurate and appropriate?

Research documentation is an integral part of the project. A designed and edited visual summary recording all research processes, critically analysing their methodologies, and seeking to locate the work in its cultural context will form the major part of the project. In some cases the process of investigation will be the project and in others the research and testing of ideas will lead to a definitive outcome or artefact.

Poynor, R. (2002) *Design Without Boundaries: Visual Communication in Transition*. London: Booth-Clibborn.

Poynor, R. (2003) *No More Rules: Graphic Design and Postmodernism*. London: Laurence King Publishing.

Poynor, R. (2007) *Obey the Giant: Life in the Image World*. 2nd edition. Basel: Birkhäuser Verlag.

Rose, G. (2006) *Visual Methodologies: An Introduction to the Interpretation of Visual Material*. London: SAGE Publications.

Schön, D. (1984) *The Reflective Practitioner: How Professionals Think in Action*. New York: Basic Books.

Tufte, E. (1997) *Visual and Statistical Thinking: Displays of Evidence for Decision Making*. New York: Graphics Press.

Wolff, J. (1993) *The Social Production of Art*. London: Palgrave Macmillan.

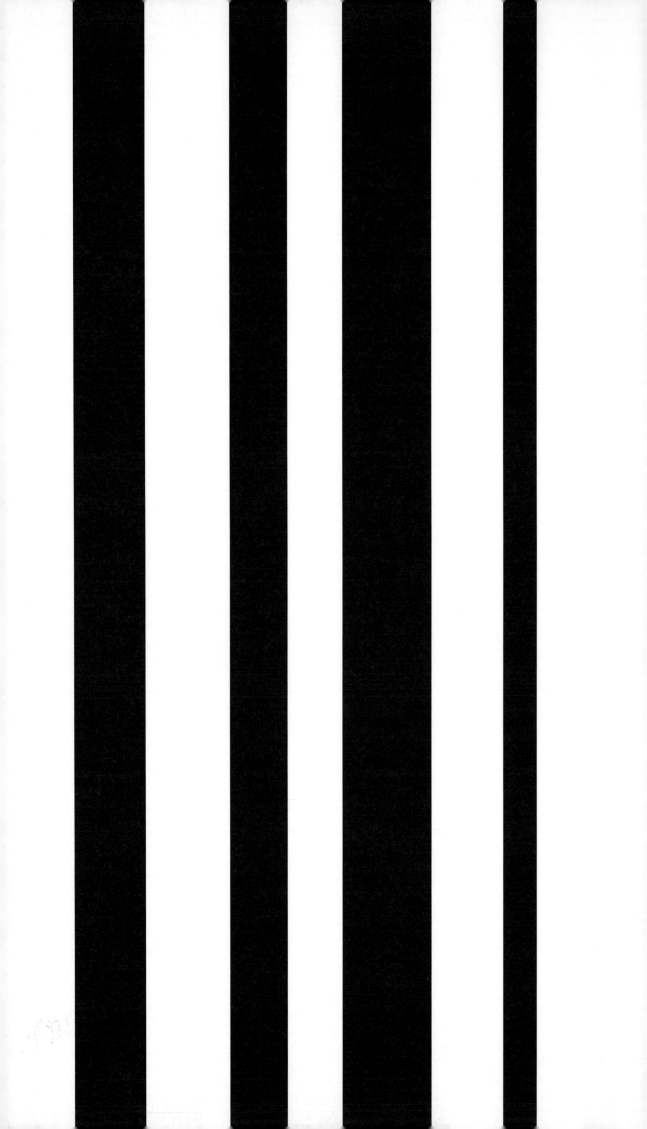

8. Appendices

Acknowledgements, Further Reading, Index and Picture Credits

WITH DRAWN

Acknowledgements

We would like to thank the staff and students, past and present, of the Postgraduate Graphic Design Programme at the London College of Communication for their critical contribution to the developments in design thinking outlined in this book. Additionally, the team at AVA Academia deserve our thanks for their support and feedback, and their patience, during the gradual evolution of this extended and completely revised edition of *Visual Research*.

Special thanks must go to the contributing designers, whose work exemplifies many of the ideas explored during the course of our work on the subject of graphic design methodologies and practice over the past decade. Their contribution to our critical thinking process should not be underestimated.

Russell Bestley would like to thank Sarah for her endless patience, support and months of lost evenings and weekends; Zobo, Nikita, Chris and of course Dad for always being there; Paul, Tony and the PGGD team at LCC for implementing and testing these ideas and theories in practice; Roger, Andrew, Stuart, Janice, Angus and the UAL Research community for inspiration and intellectual guidance; Caroline, Brian, Georgia and the AVA team; and my friends and team mates in the distance-running community for providing an outlet away from work, writing and design when I needed one. I would also like to dedicate this book in memory of Mum.

Ian Noble:
'I would like to thank myself, and congratulate myself, and if I could, I would pat myself on the back.'
Dee Dee Ramone's acceptance speech at the Ramones induction ceremony for the Rock and Roll Hall of Fame 2002.

Love as always for Susan, Eugene and Audra.

Location Photography
Sarah Dryden
Email: drydensarah@hotmail.com

Project Photography and Archive
Paul McNeil
Email: p.mcneil@lcc.arts.ac.uk

Contributing Designers

Amandine Alessandra
Email: tellme@amandinealessandra.com
Web: www.amandinealessandra.com

Gemma Dinham
Email: mail@gemmadinham.com
Web: www.gemmadinham.com

Georgia Evagorou
Email: egeorgia@cytanet.com.cy
Web: www.georgiaevagorou.com

Becky Ford
Email: hello@becky-ford.com
Web: www.becky-ford.com

Andrea Forgacs
Email: post@andreaforgacs.de
www.andreaforgacs.com

Alexandra Hayes – I Am Alexandra
Email: me@iamalexandra.com
Web: www.iamalexandra.com

Alberto Hernández – Here I Go
Email: alberto@hereigo.co.uk
Web: www.hereigo.co.uk

Charlotte Knibbs – Design Like You Give a Damn
Email: say@likeyougiveadamn.com
Web: www.likeyougiveadamn.com

Kenzo Kramarz
Email: kenzomk@kenzomk.com
Web: www.kenzomk.com

Neil Mabbs
Email: nmabbs1@btinternet.com

Orlagh O'Brien
Email: hello@orlaghobrien.com
Web: www.orlaghobrien.com
www.emotionallyvague.com

Niall O'Shea – Studio O'Shea
Email: hello@nialloshea.com
Web: www.nialloshea.com

Edouard Pecher
Email: edpech@gmail.com
Web: www.edpecher.be

Further Reading

Armstrong, H. (2009)
**Graphic Design Theory:
Readings from the Field**
New York: Princeton Architectural
Press

Batchelor, D. (2000)
Chromophobia
London: Reaktion Books

Beirut, M., Drenttel W. & Heller, S.
(1994) **Critical Writings On
Graphic Design, Volumes 1, 2, 3**
New York: Allworth Press

Bennett, A. (2006)
**Design Studies: Theory and
Research in Graphic Design**
New York: Princeton Architectural
Press

Buchanan, R. & Margolin, V. (eds.)
(1995) **Discovering Design:
Explorations in Design Studies**
Chicago: University of Chicago
Press

Cross, N. (2007)
Designerly Ways of Knowing
Basel: Birkhäuser Verlag

Crow, D. (2010)
**Visible Signs: An Introduction
to Semiotics in the Visual Arts,**
2nd edition
Worthing: AVA Publishing SA

Dondis, D. A. (1973)
A Primer of Visual Literacy
Cambridge, MA: MIT Press

Emmison, M. & Smith, P. (2000)
**Researching the Visual:
Introducing Qualitative
Methods**
London: SAGE Publications

Erlhoff, M. & Marshall, T. (eds.)
(2008) **Design Dictionary:
Perspectives on Design
Terminology**
Basel: Birkhäuser Verlag

Frascara, J. (1997)
**User-centred Graphic Design:
Mass Communications and
Social Change**
London: Taylor & Francis

Gage, J. (1995)
**Colour and Culture: Practice
and Meaning from Antiquity
to Abstraction**
London: Thames and Hudson

Harvey, C. & Press, J. (1996)
**Databases in Historical
Research: Theory, Methods and
Applications**
London: Palgrave Macmillan

Heller, S. & Finamore, M, E. (eds.)
(1997) **Design Culture: An
Anthology of Writing from the
AIGA Journal of Graphic Design**
New York: Allworth Press

Heller, S. & Pomeroy, K. (1997)
**Design Literacy: Understanding
Graphic Design**
New York: Allworth Press

Kepes, G. (1944)
Language of Vision
Chicago: Paul Theobald

Laurel, B. (ed.) (2003)
**Design Research: Methods
and Perceptions**
Cambridge, MA: MIT Press

Leborg, C. (2007)
Visual Grammar
New York: Princeton Architectural
Press

Lupton, E. & Abbott Miller, J.
(1991) **The ABC's of Bauhaus:
The Bauhaus and Design Theory**
New York: Herb Lubalin Center of
Design and Typography, Cooper
Union

Lupton, E. & Abbott Miller, J.
(2006) **Design Writing Research:
Writing on Graphic Design**
London: Phaidon

Margolin, V. (ed.) (1989)
**Design Discourse: History,
Theory, Criticism**
Chicago: University of Chicago
Press

Margolin, V. & Buchanan, R. (eds.)
(1995) **The Idea of Design: A
Design Issues Reader**
Cambridge, MA: MIT Press

Michel, R. (2007)
**Design Research Now: Essays
and Selected Projects**
Basel: Birkhäuser Verlag

Norman, D. (2002)
The Design of Everyday Things
New York: Basic Books

Poynor, R. (2003)
**No More Rules: Graphic Design
and Postmodernism**
London: Laurence King Publishing

Poynor, R. (2001)
**Obey the Giant: Life in the
Image World.** 2nd edition.
Basel: Birkhäuser Verlag

Roberts, L. & Thrift, J. (2005)
The Designer and the Grid
Brighton: RotoVision

Rose, G. (2007)
**Visual Methodologies:
An Introduction to the
Interpretation of Visual
Materials**
London: SAGE Publications

Schön, D. (1993)
**The Reflective Practitioner:
How Professionals Think in
Action**
New York: Basic Books

Swanson, G. (2000)
**Graphic Design and Reading:
Explorations of an Uneasy
Relationship**
New York: Allworth Press

Walker J. A. (1989)
**Design History and the History
of Design**
London: Pluto

Wilde, J. & R. (1991)
**Visual Literacy: A Conceptual
Approach to Solving Graphic
Problems**
New York: Watson-Guptill
Publications

Index

Index

Compiled by Indexing Specialists (UK) Ltd.

Picture Credits

Case Studies

Pages 33–35: Images from
The Square and Perspective
courtesy of Charlotte Knibbs.

Pages 36–39: Images from
Half-tone Patterns courtesy of
Niall O'Shea.

Pages 40–45: Images from
*Generative Identity / A System
of Oppositions* courtesy of
Edouard Pecher.

Pages 75–81: Images from
Emotionally Vague courtesy
of Orlagh O'Brien.

Pages 83–91: Images from
*Bibliospot / Visualising Library
Collections* courtesy of Alexandra
Hayes (née Shepherd).

Pages 107–113: Images from
The English courtesy of
Gemma Dinham.

Pages 115–123: Images from
An Inventory of Loss courtesy
of Neil Mabbs.

Pages 141–145: Images from
Hybrid Novels courtesy of
Alberto Hernández.

Pages 147–153: Images from
Representing Cypriot Identity
courtesy of Georgia Evagorou.

Pages 167–171: Images from
Mary courtesy of Andrea Forgacs.

Pages 173–181: Images from
Message as Flux courtesy of
Amandine Alessandra.

Pages 195–201: Images from
Memorial courtesy of Becky Ford.

Pages 203–209: Images from
todayifeel courtesy of Kenzo
Kramarz.

Location Photography

Pages 19, 73, 93, 103, 105, 125,
135, 136, 137, 163, 193, 211:
Photographs © Sarah Dryden.
All rights reserved.

Design and Illustrations

Visual Research, 2nd edition:
Design, Layout, Diagrams and
Illustrations © Russell Bestley
and Ian Noble. All rights reserved.